Canadians Speak on
INNOVATION
and LEARNING

CANADA'S
INNOVATION
STRATEGY

This publication is available upon request in multiple formats.
Contact the centres at the numbers listed below.

For additional copies of this publication, please contact:

Information Distribution Centre
Communications and Marketing Branch
Industry Canada
Room 268D, West Tower
235 Queen Street
Ottawa ON K1A 0H5

Tel.: (613) 947-7466
Fax: (613) 954-6436
E-mail: **publications@ic.gc.ca**

Enquiries Centre
Human Resources Development Canada
140 Promenade du Portage
Phase IV, Level O
Gatineau QC KIA 0J9

Fax: (819) 953-7260
E-mail: **pub@hrdc-drhc.gc.ca**

This publication is also available electronically on the World Wide Web at the following address:
http://www.innovationstrategy.gc.ca

Permission to Reproduce

Except as otherwise specifically noted, the information in this publication may be reproduced, in part or in whole and by any means, without charge or further permission from Industry Canada or Human Resources Development Canada, provided that due diligence is exercised in ensuring the accuracy of the information reproduced; that Industry Canada and Human Resources Development Canada are identified as the source institutions; and that the reproduction is not represented as an official version of the information reproduced, nor as having been made in affiliation with, or with the endorsement of, Industry Canada and Human Resources Development Canada.

For permission to reproduce the information in this publication for commercial redistribution, please e-mail:
copyright.droitdauteur@communication.gc.ca

Cat. No. Iu4-21/2002
ISBN 0-662-66955-X
53818B

10% recycled
material

CONTENTS

FOREWORD

Canadians Speak on Innovation and Learning highlights the key points and perspectives of a large number of Canadian organizations that answered the Government of Canada's "call to action" in the *Innovation Strategy* papers released in February 2002. *Achieving Excellence: Investing in People, Knowledge and Opportunity* and *Knowledge Matters: Skills and Learning for Canadians* laid out a number of challenges facing Canada in the journey to becoming one of the most innovative and skilled countries in the world from an economic and social perspective — a country with world-class research facilities, companies and communities, and a talented, mobile, healthy and committed work force. The two papers were intended to act as a catalyst for discussion on challenges and milestones related to research and development and commercialization, skills and learning, immigration, an innovation-friendly business climate, and communities that act as magnets for talent and investment.

From May 2002 to October 2002, the Government of Canada engaged key stakeholders from a wide range of large and small businesses; academia; governments; industry, business and labour organizations; voluntary sector organizations; and other stakeholders and partners in a series of regional, national, and sectoral meetings, expert roundtables, and best practice events, to solicit feedback on and commitment to *Canada's Innovation Strategy*. In addition to the 10 000 Canadians who participated across the country, several hundred provided their individual comments using on-line tools. There were more than 250 formal written submissions from companies and organizations covering a broad and diverse range of Canadian business and social society. The reports from engagement activities and the submissions are the basis of this report, which is, in essence, a summary of "what we heard" over the past few months.

Readers interested in an overview of the shared priorities and suggested actions arising from all of the streams of the engagement process are directed to Chapter 10.

The Government of Canada thanks all Canadians who participated in the engagement process and who brought forward their views on this important initiative. A list of organizations that provided input, as well as many of their formal reports and submissions, can be viewed on the *Innovation Strategy* Web site (**www.innovationstrategy.gc.ca**).

MINISTERS' MESSAGE

On February 12, 2002, we officially launched *Canada's Innovation Strategy.* In the 10 months that followed, our departments and our partners organized over 80 sectoral meetings, 33 regional summits, a rural summit and 20 roundtable discussions. In addition to the 250 formal submissions we received, we heard from 1000 young people, while more than 600 small and medium-sized enterprises and individual Canadians contributed their reactions on-line. As you will see in the pages that follow, the diversity of opinions presented is very striking. It is precisely the wide range of views offered that has made these discussions so valuable.

We wish to thank the more than 10 000 Canadians who participated in these engagement activities. Throughout the engagement process, the "people" aspect of innovation has been emphasized. Canadians understand that it is people who innovate, people who create ideas, and people who implement those ideas. We commend each and every participant for their commitment to this national vision and for the insightful advice they have provided.

Innovation and learning are crucial to a high standard of living for Canadians. The Government of Canada can create the kind of environment in which innovation can flourish, but the government cannot forge a common strategy to address the innovation challenge by itself. For this, it needed the input and advice of people in all regions and from all sectors of the economy. In particular, we needed to hear from the private sector, which is a key driver of innovation and creator of jobs.

At the National Summit on Innovation and Learning, delegates representing our partners, the private sector, the voluntary sector, educational institutions, unions, other levels of government and individuals will be prioritizing the recommendations for action that emerged during the engagement process. We will also be sharing ideas on what actions are required within those priority areas to address the challenges discussed in *Knowledge Matters* and *Achieving Excellence* — the two papers that comprise *Canada's Innovation Strategy*. Clearly, the Summit will be a milestone event in this long-term strategy, where we will be moving from verification and refinement of the challenges facing Canada to building the foundation for a national action plan that will guide our growth for the next decade.

What has been achieved during the engagement process is inspiring: many strong new relationships have been developed and effective new partnerships established. It has become clear that, as a nation, we share a common vision. We appreciate the power and importance of an innovative culture and a highly skilled work force in a modern Canada. *Canadians Speak on Innovation and Learning* is an important legacy of this engagement process.

Together, we can ensure that we are equipped with the tools we need for Canada to become one of the most innovative countries in the world. By embarking on a national project, we can support innovation in all regions and ensure the full participation of all Canadians.

Allan Rock
Minister of Industry

Jane Stewart
Minister of Human Resources
Development

CHAPTER 1

INTRODUCTION

WHY AN INNOVATION STRATEGY?

Innovation is about people coming up with new ideas and putting them to work. It means having the right people with the right skills to produce things better, faster and cheaper, bringing new products to market, and finding new markets for goods and services.

> *"Harnessing the innovative capacity of Canadians requires the ability to look beyond where we are today, and to build a dream that sets the stage for the future."*
>
> Paul Bush,
> Vice-President Corporate Development, Telesat Canada,
> Chair of Space Sector Roundtable

Stepping up the scope and pace of innovation in all sectors of the economy and society will improve Canadians' standard of living, protect our enviable quality of life and ensure that all citizens have the opportunity to benefit from a more innovative and productive society. *Canada's Innovation Strategy* is a way to prepare Canadians for the 21st century, to provide a vision and a sequence of objectives and actions that all members of the economy and society can work together to address.

The strategy papers

Canada's Innovation Strategy is a work in progress. It was launched in February 2002 by the Ministers of Industry and Human Resources Development with the release of two strategy papers. The strategy papers are intended to set out the economic, social and demographic context behind Canada's innovation and learning challenges, and to identify some of the reasons why our performance trails many other industrialized countries. They also set out medium- and long-term goals and objectives that, taken together, describe what Canada may look like in the future if all of the stakeholders in the economy and society joined in a national effort to build a culture of innovation and learning. The targets set for the agenda span to 2010. Highlights of the two strategy papers and details on the proposed goals and milestones are presented in the Appendix, Sections I and II.

Achieving Excellence: Investing in People, Knowledge and Opportunity was prepared by Industry Canada. The paper looks at the innovation process in detail — how and where people, ideas, and capital come together to commercialize and market new products and processes. It sets out goals and targets, and poses important questions in four areas:

1. Knowledge Performance: How can we increase investment in research and development (R&D) and bring promising ideas to market more quickly?

2. Skills: How can we ensure that Canada has enough highly qualified people to drive innovation in all sectors of the economy?

3. Innovation Environment: How can we create regulations and a tax system that balance the public interest with the competitive pressures faced by Canadian firms?

4. Strengthening Communities: How can we stimulate innovation at the local level to ensure that people in all parts of Canada have the opportunity to participate in the knowledge-based economy?

Knowledge Matters: Skills and Learning for Canadians was prepared by Human Resources Development Canada (HRDC). It deals with the human capital side of the innovation formula — how to keep up with the ever-rising demand for skills and address looming demographic challenges to ensure that Canada maintains a world-class work force. The paper also sets out goals and milestones, and poses important questions in four areas:

1. Children and Youth: How can we give young people the best possible start and ensure that they are ready for lifelong learning?

2. Post-Secondary Education: How can we ensure that Canadians have access to apprenticeship programs, college and university study, including graduate programs?

3. The Adult Labour Force: How can we ensure that Canadians already working continue to upgrade their knowledge and abilities and adapt to changing technology and skill requirements?

4. Immigration: How can we ensure that Canada continues to attract highly skilled immigrants and helps them to achieve their full potential in our society and labour market?

Knowledge Matters and *Achieving Excellence* issued a "call to action." They invited all Canadians to come together to develop an action plan for innovation and learning and to articulate a shared vision of the future for Canadians. The first step in this process was one of engagement. This part of the process will culminate in a National Summit on Innovation and Learning in Toronto, November 18–19, 2002.

THE ENGAGEMENT PROCESS

In May 2002, Minister Rock and Minister Stewart launched an engagement process on behalf of the Government of Canada to animate discussion on Canada's innovation and learning challenges among large and small businesses, industry sectors, national business associations, youth, Aboriginal peoples, academic and research institutions, municipalities, economic development organizations, sector councils,[1] labour groups, communities, and regions. The Government of Canada engaged provincial and territorial governments in discussions on *Canada's Innovation Strategy* through a parallel process involving a series of meetings and events. The overall objective was to bring a large number of Canadians into the discussion, solicit their feedback and ideas on the targets and proposed actions, and challenge them to develop their own action plans to enhance innovation and learning performance. In particular, the Government of Canada asked:

• Are the goals and objectives, targets and milestones set out in *Achieving Excellence* and *Knowledge Matters* properly framed? Are they reasonable and achievable?

---

1. *Sector councils bring together employers, unions and other employee representatives with the education and training community to identify and respond to human resource challenges. They have become important players in the labour market and now operate in 26 industries (representing 25 percent of the work force), ranging from steel, mining and textiles to aerospace, construction and tourism.*

- Are the options for action well conceived? Will they contribute significantly to influencing the necessary changes in Canada's innovation and learning performance within the specified time frames?

- What are the principal barriers to innovation and learning in Canada? What actions will overcome these obstacles?

- What roles and responsibilities should business, education and training providers, labour, communities and governments accept in building a more innovative and skilled Canada? What is each player best suited to do?

Over the last six months, stakeholders were invited to take part in government-wide discussions about innovation and learning. Engagement events and meetings took place from coast to coast to coast; in large cities and small communities. They involved organizations and individuals with a very wide range of backgrounds, interests and perspectives. HRDC and Industry Canada took the lead in these discussions using several different approaches.

HRDC engaged more than 1200 stakeholders through 10 best practice workshops, six expert roundtables and a series of bilateral meetings. The purposes of the best practice workshops were to document lessons learned, share best practices and emerging approaches, and develop a stronger national dialogue on skills and learning issues. Each workshop focussed on a specific subject area that could be part of a national approach to skills and learning. The subjects were: e-learning; sector councils; apprenticeships; a labour market strategy for people with disabilities; building learning communities; innovation in workplace skills and learning; literacy; immigrants and the labour market; learning recognition; and

knowledge and information on skills and learning. The expert roundtables concentrated on consulting with key stakeholders about their priorities for skills and learning, and identifying possible actions to achieve the goals set out in *Knowledge Matters*. About 50 stakeholders participated in each event, each of which focussed on a specific population group and the skills and learning challenges they face. The topics of the roundtable deliberations were: adult learners' access to post-secondary education; youth; Aboriginal peoples; the adult labour force; children; and Canadians' overall access to post-secondary education, and the capacity issues in the system.

In addition, HRDC also invited individuals and organizations to provide input on the goals and milestones set out in *Knowledge Matters* by using its on-line "Public Engagement Workbooks."

At Industry Canada, the engagement process unfolded along sectoral, regional and industry streams. Some 70 industries provided feedback on *Achieving Excellence* and *Knowledge Matters* through formal submissions. National business associations, economic development organizations and other groups provided their views in similar fora. The department sponsored, along with HRDC, "regional summits" in 33 communities across Canada, and invited the public to provide additional views using the on-line "Do It Yourself Kits." A rural summit was also organized and smaller roundtables were held in some provinces. A special on-line survey was used to reach small and medium-sized enterprises. Both HRDC and Industry Canada sought input from youth and Aboriginal groups during the engagement process.

In addition, other federal government departments were invited to join in engaging their stakeholder groups across the country in innovation- and learning-related discussions. Meetings were held with Health Canada, Natural Resources Canada, Transport Canada, Agriculture and Agri-Food Canada, Canadian Heritage, Environment Canada, Citizenship and Immigration Canada, the Department of Foreign Affairs and International Trade, Fisheries and Oceans Canada, the Department of Finance Canada, the Department of Justice Canada, the Rural Secretariat, Status of Women Canada, and Communication Canada, as well as with the National Research Council Canada, the federal granting councils, the Canadian Institutes of Health Research, Communications Research Centre Canada, the Office of International Partnerships Canada, and others. Several of these departments and agencies held their own engagement meetings with client groups to solicit reactions to the *Innovation Strategy*.

The material and information gathered through this comprehensive process has resulted in a growing body of knowledge that will be an important resource as policy and decision makers across the public and private sectors move *Canada's Innovation Strategy* forward in the months ahead. As well, enthusiasm for the vision put forward in *Canada's Innovation Strategy* has been growing and will form a strong base for the development of an action plan on innovation and learning.

All told, more than 10 000 people from business; trade unions; education and training providers; the Aboriginal community; young people; provincial, territorial and municipal governments; and not-for-profit and other groups shared their thoughts and concerns about the *Innovation Strategy*. Some 250 groups and organizations expressed their views in formal reports that ran to more than 3000 pages. In addition, more than 500 small businesses completed on-line questionnaires, and thousands of individuals and community groups joined the engagement process by e-mail, through phone calls or by completing and returning "Do It Yourself Kits" and "Public Engagement Workbooks."

All of this input has been compiled to identify the major issues of concern to a broad range of Canadians and stakeholder groups, and to highlight their views and recommendations on Canada's innovation and learning challenges. Some of these recommendations are targeted specifically for action by governments, but Canadians are very clear about the need for a coordinated, multi-partnered strategy with every sector taking responsibility for action. This includes the education community, non-governmental organizations, private firms of all sizes, business and industry associations, municipalities, libraries, science centres, technology transfer centres, economic development organizations, and community groups. One of the key messages that emerged encouraged new forms of collaborative arrangements and partnerships — highlighting the need to work together in new ways and to strengthen the environment for innovation in Canada.

ABOUT THIS DOCUMENT

Canadians Speak on Innovation and Learning captures the thoughts, suggestions and concerns expressed by Canadians through this process. It is intended to be a summary of views that will help shape a 10–year strategy. The vast majority of the individual reports that make up this document are available for on-line public viewing at the *Innovation Strategy* Web site (**www.innovationstrategy.gc.ca**).

> **"Anyone can innovate. Innovation**
>
> **is for all Canadians."**

Ocean Technologies (Pacific) Industry Innovation Committee

The following chapters summarize what different groups of Canadians ("streams of engagement") had to say in relation to the key challenge areas and themes set out in the strategy papers, namely R&D and commercialization; the learning and immigration systems; skills; taxation and regulation; and community innovative capacity.

Chapter 2 summarizes the conclusions and recommendations of 33 regional summits organized by Industry Canada and HRDC, and of a rural summit organized by the Rural Secretariat in cooperation with Industry Canada and HRDC. More than 5000 representatives from business, government, the not-for-profit sector, the research and education communities, and community leaders took part in these meetings. Integrated in this chapter are the additional perspectives of more than 100 individuals who submitted their views on-line.

Chapter 3 expresses the views of more than 1000 young Canadians who took part in a number of roundtable discussions and other events. It reflects the hopes, aspirations and concerns of tomorrow's leaders and Canada's future work force, whose main priorities are skills and learning.

Chapter 4 reflects the ideas and concerns of Aboriginal Canadians. These came from the views of more than 500 Aboriginal men and women who took part in regional summits, roundtables and best practices workshops. Their views were supplemented by information provided in formal submissions from Aboriginal business, economic development and health-oriented organizations.

Chapter 5 summarizes the views of four different groups: national business associations that speak on behalf of hundreds of individual firms; economic development organizations, which work at the local level to promote industrial and employment growth; labour organizations, which represent hundreds of Canadian workers; and sector councils, a consortia of business, labour and academia that address human resource challenges in 26 industries.

Chapter 6 pulls together the views of some 80 industry sectors. Part A describes what we heard from a broad cross-section of sectors, ranging from resource-based and traditional manufacturing and service activities to the emerging fields of life and environmental sciences and nanotechnology. Part B highlights what we heard from the information and communication technology sector, which includes views from telecommunications companies, supplier firms, and users. The separate treatment of the information and communication technology sector in this chapter reflects its role as an enabling force in innovation, and the significant role it plays in Canada's current R&D performance.

Chapter 7 presents the findings of an on-line survey through which small and medium-sized enterprises from all parts of the country were invited to submit their views. Almost 500 owners of small firms shared their opinions on what they see as Canada's innovation priorities.

Chapter 8 provides feedback from the academic community — the people and organizations at the heart of Canada's learning and knowledge creation systems, frequently referred to as the "nucleus of an innovation system." These include representatives from universities, colleges, libraries, research institutes, and school boards, as well as faculty associations, student associations, learners and education advocacy groups.

Chapter 9 reports on the outcomes of government-to-government discussions with provinces and territories on *Canada's Innovation Strategy*.

Chapter 10 highlights the main priorities that generated consensus across engagement streams and summarizes the major suggested actions and recommendations brought forward or endorsed through the engagement process.

The Appendix presents a summary of the major goals, targets and milestones laid out in *Achieving Excellence* and *Knowledge Matters* in February 2002.

NEW OPPORTUNITIES FOR PARTNERSHIP

It is important to remind readers that addressing Canada's innovation and learning challenges is a long-term national approach that entails the development of priorities and actions. In the *Innovation Strategy* papers, the Government of Canada proposes actions that could be undertaken, and commits to working with provinces and territories and other partners to meet stated goals and targets to address the major challenges. These collaborative efforts will position Canada as the best place in the world to live and work, and as a leader in such areas as R&D investment, commercialization and skills development. Clearly, provincial and territorial governments are essential partners in helping to create and sustain this stronger innovation and culture in Canada. With responsibilities in education and training, work force development, taxation, securities regulation, and a host of other policy areas that directly affect innovation performance, they are key players. Provincial and territorial governments are already committing significant resources to foster innovation and expand skills and learning opportunities. All of them agree that more needs to be done, fiscal capacity permitting.

Municipal government policies also affect the ability to attract the capital and human resources that drive innovation, so local authorities must also be part of the picture. The Federation of Canadian Municipalities has been actively involved in the engagement process and presented its views to the Government of Canada on priorities to reduce the innovation and learning gap in Canadian communities. Recent discussions may ultimately lead to new partnerships geared to improving the innovative capacity of communities.

The interest to partner in a shared vision of a more innovative and skilled Canada, as expressed by provincial and territorial governments, universities and colleges, labour organizations, private R&D performers, municipalities, the voluntary sector and community economic development groups, to name only a few, is evidence of the readiness of Canadians to move forward.

CHAPTER 2

WHAT WE HEARD FROM PEOPLE IN CANADA'S REGIONS

THE ENGAGEMENT PROCESS

Between May and early October 2002, day-long summit meetings were held in 33 communities across Canada to discuss proposed innovation priorities and targets, and to recommend actions that could improve regional innovation performance. A special summit was organized to bring forward the views of rural communities, emphasizing the particular challenges faced in rural, remote and Northern regions. A number of smaller roundtables were held in some provinces. Each summit and roundtable involved representatives from business, education, research institutions, not-for-profit organizations and governments, as well as citizens and community leaders. HRDC held roundtables and best practices workshops to discuss specific issues related to learning communities. A workshop was held in Ottawa in June 2002 on labour market issues for persons with disabilities, and provided perspectives from this community. Finally, individual citizens provided their views on both the *Knowledge Matters* and *Achieving Excellence* documents using on-line consultation tools. In total, more than 5000 Canadians participated in this part of the engagement processes.

GENERAL IMPRESSIONS

There was widespread consensus on the need for action. With very few exceptions, communities and individual citizens strongly agreed with *Achieving Excellence* and *Knowledge Matters* on the challenges Canada faces. Participants supported the basic premise that Canada needs to develop a broad-based culture of innovation, and that this means developing more collaborative partnerships between, among and across governments, sectors of the economy, educational and research institutions of all types, and communities. Coming through loud and clear was the view that innovation is not synonymous with high technology, science or research alone — that it is equally important to be innovative in all sectors of the economy, and in "capacity-building" fields such as education, health and social services. In regional events and roundtable sessions, many Canadians expressed a strong desire to follow up on ideas generated during discussions. Communities were enthusiastic about developing community plans for innovation. They see government as fostering an environment to allow individual communities to move forward with integrated innovation strategies.

There was also widespread recognition of the need for flexibility — for a national approach to improving Canada's innovation performance that would play to the particular strengths and address the distinct needs of communities and regions — acknowledging that "one size fits all" won't work. This was evident from the differing perspectives of participants in large urban centres versus those in rural and smaller remote communities. Summits in urban centres tended to emphasize the challenges of access to sufficient, long-term funding and venture capital to accelerate R&D and commercialization, and applying innovations to improve productivity. Rural, Northern and remote centres, meanwhile, focussed on "entry-level" needs, such as basic infrastructure requirements and broadband connectivity, on increasing opportunities for youth in order to stem out-migration, and on incentives to retain skilled people. In short, while large centres wanted to build on what they have and improve their ability to compete in the global economy, smaller centres were looking for support to keep what they have and become part of the global economy.

All regions took a broad view of innovation. There was strong support for improving tax incentives for technology development and adoption, and improving access to risk and venture capital, particularly for small and medium-sized enterprises at the commercialization stage. In at least three regions, summit participants called for improvements to research infrastructure and funding. They highlighted the need for more partnerships and stronger relationships between academic researchers and businesses to facilitate the transfer of technology; greater efforts to attract and accelerate the approval and accreditation of skilled immigrants; action to reduce government red tape and speed up regulatory reform, particularly to support small and medium-sized enterprises; one-stop access to innovation programs and services; and a realignment of the education system to support

innovation and expose young people to entrepreneurial opportunities. In summits held in rural and northern communities, participants stressed the importance of Aboriginal and Inuit people participating fully in the new economy.

The workshop that focussed on issues affecting persons with disabilities stressed the importance of viewing this population, along with newcomers to Canada, as a key source of the skilled labour Canada needs. The key role of assistive devices was emphasized, as these not only represent innovations in their own right, but offer tremendous potential to increase access for persons with disabilities to learning opportunities in post-secondary education institutions and the workplace, and, thereby, facilitate their participation in the knowledge economy.

From the responses of citizens who provided their individual input through on-line consultation tools, a strong focus on supporting small and medium-sized enterprises and increasing their access to venture capital was also in evidence. They supported actions to increase investments in education, including those to promote wider access to post-secondary education and to encourage workplace-based training and lifelong learning. They recommended mentoring programs, more apprenticeships and increased efforts to recognize international credentials and remove barriers to immigrants' integration into the labour market. Citizens also asked for affordable broadband access, and for government to do more to combat the risk-averse nature of the Canadian mindset by promoting innovation successes and raising Canadians' overall awareness of, and confidence in, our innovation potential.

The input from Canada's regions on the four priority areas — skills and learning, research, development and commercialization, the innovation environment, and communities — follows.

Aligning the learning system to reflect labour market needs

This was the central concern driving most of the recommendations made by summit and roundtable participants across the country, as well as many submissions from individual citizens. They repeatedly stressed the need for improved access to post-secondary education to overcome geographic and cost barriers; improved promotion of opportunities in skilled trades; and action to increase access to adult education and workplace training. Improving the alignment of post-secondary education, training and lifelong learning programs with the skill requirements of the labour market was seen as involving more mentorships, apprenticeships, internships and fellowships. In British Columbia, participants called for increasing "authentic workplace experiences" in learning by strengthening co-op education programs and apprenticeships. In Edmonton, participants felt the Government of Canada is too focussed on university education. Indeed, a common thread across all regions was a strong recommendation to include colleges, technical schools and the skilled trades as key components of the innovation learning system.

" We believe that establishing a new Internet technology apprenticeship program would help double the number of apprentices completing a certification program over the next decade."

Computing Technology Industry Association

In Prince Edward Island, participants suggested intergovernmental cooperation to encourage lifelong learning and improved skills development through their province's Labour Market Development Agreement with the federal government. In Newfoundland and Regina, participants recommended expanding employment insurance to cover skills and training for employed workers. Targets for education and training across a range of institutions and programs were suggested in Nova Scotia, and, in New Brunswick and Alberta, participants suggested lessening the burden imposed by additional fees for foreign post-secondary education students and eliminating restrictions on international students. In Nunavut, where 40 percent of the population is under 15 years of age, participants stressed the need for an approach to skills and learning that responds to their demographic realities, and that supports a critical mass of learning and training that can feed into the local economy.

Engaging industry directly in curriculum development was suggested in Winnipeg, and, in Calgary, participants called for more partnerships and alliances between educational organizations and the private sector. In Windsor, participants suggested matching the curricula and equipment used in schools to current industry standards. Tax incentives for employers and individuals were seen everywhere as key instruments to promote skills upgrading and lifelong learning. Support for distance learning and broadband connectivity were viewed as key measures to overcome access barriers. In Northern Ontario, participants called for more efforts to improve the quality of adult education and training and, in Niagara, participants suggested scholarships for education in the skilled trades.

Again, interjurisdictional tensions and rivalry, and a lack of federal–provincial cooperation, along with too much competition between governments and between educational institutions, were seen in most regions as major barriers to making the strategic investments Canada needs in education, training, and recognition of credentials.

A strong emphasis was placed on the responsibility of employers to do more in the workplace. Participants felt that, too often, employers view their human resource/learning expenditures as a cost rather than an investment or benefit. On the other hand, the business community stressed the need to remember the realities of the business cycle, the differences between industry sectors, and the need to be able to deliver economies of scale to small and medium-sized enterprises. There was strong support for a role for sector councils in this area.

Recognition of workplace learning was also seen as a key element of the skills and learning architecture. One of the main obstacles that participants raised was the lack of interprovincial recognition of workplace learning. Participants embraced the possibility of the development of national standards and national tools for the recognition of workplace learning, and stressed that achieving this will require the commitment and leadership of government, industry, sector councils, educational institutions, and others.

There was also consensus that Canada needs to increase the number of apprenticeships, an issue that participants stressed has been around for at least the last 10 years. They see an "image problem" as an overarching issue, and said that a long-term strategy needs to sell apprenticeships as viable career options. They also added that entry into an apprenticeship is often too difficult, especially for immigrants, limiting Canada's ability to take full advantage of the specialized trades and occupational skills that immigrants bring with them to this country.

Work force inclusion

In all regions, summit participants raised the need to address barriers facing key groups such as persons with disabilities, Aboriginal people and immigrants. Repeatedly, they stressed the need for strategies to attract and retain highly qualified immigrants, and to speed up the integration of foreign talent into the domestic labour market by improving the system of recognition for foreign credentials. However, according to input from individual citizens, many felt that focussing solely on highly educated immigrants was unjust and could discriminate against those in the skilled trades or without official credentials. They wanted an assessment of the "whole person," and several submissions called for more funding for language training and settlement services. In Toronto, a parallel innovation strategy for Aboriginal people, with a focus on youth, was recommended.

The need to maximize the contributions of all segments of society was emphasized in Quebec, where participants urged that the *Innovation Strategy* should take account of the fact that baby boomers will begin to retire in record numbers, taking their skills and knowledge with them at a time when the demand for skilled labour will be increasing. This "soon to retire" cohort was also identified as a key source of mentors.

Submissions from individual citizens repeatedly referenced barriers to adult learning and skills development, notably time and cost. More and better e-learning was suggested, as was encouraging employers to do more to accommodate workers' learning needs. Many of these submissions called for self-assessment tools, so that adults could identify their learning needs themselves, and a standardized accreditation process, so that they could be sure they are accessing high-quality skills, learning programs and services. Other individual citizens suggested making post-secondary education 100 percent publicly funded, earmarking a specific amount of the Canada Health and Social Transfer (to provinces and territories) for education, and encouraging employers to provide loans to students.

RESEARCH, DEVELOPMENT AND COMMERCIALIZATION

Research and development

In all regions, summit participants called for improved coordination and more collaboration between industry, academia and governments in funding research and research infrastructure, and for a more integrated and coordinated approach to policy and regulations affecting research. They also felt that fostering an investment environment conducive to innovation was critical in order to generate the knowledge, through pure and applied research, upon which innovation relies.

In Atlantic Canada, summit participants said that targets were hard to understand and lacked specificity. In Nova Scotia, they recommended better regional representation on national research funding bodies. In Quebec, participants strongly stressed the need to recognize the innovation potential in traditional and resource-based industries, which are the lifeblood for some communities, analogous to the way high technology is recognized in major centres. In Newfoundland, participants stressed the importance of encouraging research and innovation in the resource sector, and of providing research funding and support to smaller universities to help keep educated young people in the communities and regions that need their talent to generate knowledge. This point was reinforced in New Brunswick, where participants also pointed to the need for more financial support for universities to fund the indirect costs related to university research. In rural and northern areas of Ontario, summit participants highlighted the roles of transportation systems and infrastructure, particularly broadband access, to enabling knowledge creation. Streamlined access to research funding was also suggested, along with a fairer balance between pure and applied research.

Participants in all regions repeatedly raised the issue of lack of coordination between different levels of government in knowledge creation. Significant levels of frustration were in evidence over perceived jurisdictional conflicts. In Windsor, participants noted the lack of intergovernmental coordination is what has lead to unnecessarily complex delivery structures, poor accountability and conflicting agendas. In Hamilton, participants linked this issue to interprovincial trade barriers and a pronounced lack of institutional flexibility. In Toronto, where a lack of coordination between and within federal departments was cited as a barrier to knowledge performance, participants stressed the need to clarify and harmonize programs at all levels of government, and to simplify access to them. In Calgary, participants mentioned the silos within which governments and universities work, and, in Saskatoon, participants said there are too many funding streams for research, resulting in too much money going into administration instead of research. Participants in Winnipeg agreed that the lack of collaboration between federal and provincial funding programs for research impedes progress, and in Thunder Bay/Sudbury and Vancouver, participants asked for a one-stop shop providing access to research funding, with counselors to help businesses understand the application processes for government programs.

In Calgary and Regina, participants agreed that the social dimension is missing from the proposed *Innovation Strategy*, and that social innovation is critical, particularly to ensure the participation of disadvantaged segments of the population, such as Aboriginal people and newcomers to Canada. In northern communities, participants emphasized the need to better educate Canadians about the North in order to attract people who will appreciate what it has to offer.

Commercialization

Providing more and better incentives to apply innovations, particularly through tax measures, was mentioned most often as a recommendation. A tax system that promotes and rewards innovation was seen as key to commercialization success. In Kitchener–Waterloo–Guelph, participants recommended greater incentives for the commercialization of world-first innovations. In Thunder Bay/Sudbury, participants suggested R&D tax incentives for small and medium-sized enterprises.

Again and again, participants pointed to the inadequate access to capital, particularly for small and medium-sized enterprises. In Windsor, participants agreed that Canada has a pronounced lack of "risk-tolerant" lenders, and, both in Windsor and Eastern Ontario, participants stressed that Canada needs more "patient capital," because the time horizon over which adequate financial support can be obtained is at least as important as the amount of that support. This point was also stressed in the Ottawa/Gatineau summit. In Nova Scotia, one of the recommendations was to foster an investment environment that supports high risk and high investment in the period leading to commercialization. This need for risk financing was echoed in several of the Quebec summits.

More support for technology transfer through increased cooperation between universities and industry was also a common recommendation at all the regional summits. This theme was further evident in submissions from individuals, with suggestions that government should create a separately funded organization to facilitate the commercialization of university research, and that commercial researchers should be more involved in academic research.

INNOVATION ENVIRONMENT

While suggestions concerning tax and regulatory reform were made in all regional summits, participants tended to take a broad view of what constitutes a positive innovation environment. In Northern Ontario, for example, participants spoke of the need for cultural amenities and a high overall quality of life to attract the people who drive innovation. The need for an innovation culture was often referenced as important.

There were several suggestions to improve Canadians' understanding of what constitutes intellectual property. In the majority of regional summits, participants called for a change in the tax and regulatory environment to better support and reward all forms of innovation and entrepreneurship.

" Canada lags behind the United States in providing tax incentives to micro-businesses and individuals. Innovation is born in the mind of a person — not in corporate boardrooms. Individuals must be given the incentive and relief to innovate, then corporate boardrooms can act."

Private citizen submission

Infrastructure was also seen as critical to the innovation environment, particularly high-speed broadband access and local transportation systems. In the North, participants pointed to even more fundamental infrastructure needs such as more computers and affordable connectivity. More support for entrepreneurs was also suggested, including assistance with business planning, information on accessing financing, and marketing assistance.

Tax measures

In every region, summit participants spoke about the need to introduce new and more effective tax-based incentives to facilitate innovation, often along with the need to cut red tape and harmonize regulatory regimes between all three levels of government. In Newfoundland, participants called for the reform of tax regimes in order to attract new investors and venture capitalists, and, in Nova Scotia, participants suggested a tax credit for angel investors. Quebec participants recommended harmonizing innovation policies across jurisdictions, and simplifying the R&D tax credit program to make it accessible to a broader range of firms. Participants also suggested creating tax incentives to attract researchers and teaching faculty from abroad.

In Ontario, it was felt that the tax regime must be aligned within a global context to ensure that enterprises in Canada can be internationally competitive. However, in smaller communities in that province, and in other rural and northern communities, participants called for more competitive tax rates as compared to larger centres, to compensate for the higher costs of doing business. In addition to tax breaks and credits for investors, participants suggested creating technology research parks and tax-free zones to help move innovation from the laboratory to the marketplace, and establishing training tax credits to encourage the development of the human capital that

innovation requires. The call for tax reform was not restricted to the federal government. For example, in Edmonton, participants suggested that the Government of Alberta should match federal R&D tax credits and Industrial Research Assistance Program contributions.

Regulatory reform

In general, the 2010 target was seen as too long-term for urgently needed regulatory reforms. Participants in all regions wanted faster action from governments in this area, which was seen as crucial in order for government to do a better job keeping pace with innovation-driven businesses. Participants in Kitchener–Waterloo–Guelph suggested that a review of regulatory regimes affecting business begin within the next three months. Streamlining regulations between jurisdictions was also seen as a way that governments could help fast-track the commercialization of good ideas.

In Newfoundland, participants called for governments to move away from prescriptive regulatory regimes towards performance-based regulation, and, in Nova Scotia, the suggestion was made that all four Atlantic provinces harmonize their regulatory regimes. In Windsor, participants suggested that lack of harmonization with U.S. regulations was a barrier to innovation, and, in Hamilton, international and interprovincial trade barriers were cited as major impediments to innovation. In Toronto, the misalignment of federal and provincial regulatory policies, including in immigration, was identified as a barrier to innovation. The need to develop international benchmarks was seen as important in order to support regulatory modernization. In Saskatoon, participants called for an innovative regulatory system and, in Winnipeg, participants said that, once government created the right regulatory environment, the marketplace could do the rest.

STRENGTHENING COMMUNITIES

Across all regions, in addition to the unanimous endorsement for the target of extending broadband access to all parts of Canada, there was strong support for attending to the basic infrastructure (such as roads, schools and hospitals), that underpins innovation. There was also a call to balance investments in telecommunications infrastructure with these basic requirements. In British Columbia, the Prairies, Quebec, Northern Ontario and Atlantic Canada, this was seen in the context of overcoming the inherent disadvantages of having a dispersed population. At the same time, while "bricks and mortar" infrastructure was a common theme, so too was the need to focus on unleashing people talent, particularly among disadvantaged groups, and in rural parts of the country.

Rural summit participants cited the lack of physical and social infrastructure as a major barrier to economic development. These communities need special efforts to encourage and support innovative educational and training activities to overcome the lack of skill development opportunities for youth, professionals and tradespersons. Leaders from rural and Northern communities supported the continuation of Community Access Programs and called for increased efforts to foster networks and collaboration across academia, government and business.

Building learning communities

Several HRDC workshops encouraged participants to discuss the specific concept of learning communities. These could be either a geographical area or a community of interest that uses lifelong learning as an organizing principle to prepare for the knowledge-based economy. Learning communities would mobilize knowledge, skills and, in some cases, technologies, to achieve community objectives in learning, such as enhancing the skills of community residents to reduce disparities and socio-economic divisions. As communities develop their capacities, the overall quality of life of Canada would be enhanced.

Participants suggested that achieving sustainable socio-economic development benefiting all citizens could be done by fostering and organizing a community's formal and non-formal learning resources in ways that suit community purposes. Rather than focussing solely on the important period of formal schooling, learning communities integrate the links between non-formal and formal learning to recognize and value learning in all its forms throughout an individual's life, and in all settings, including at home, in the community and in the workplace. Nurturing lifelong learning is viewed as a responsibility of the entire community, including all levels of government, businesses, community groups and labour — not just education institutions, which often have a narrower view of learning.

Participants felt that, often, a lack of recognition of skills acquired outside formal structures limits an individual's prospects. Prior learning assessments and recognition of international credentials would remove some of these barriers to further learning and skills development.

A repeated theme was the need to promote social inclusion so that all citizens, including people with disabilities, single parents, Aboriginal people, recent immigrants, the working poor, and employment insurance and social assistance recipients, can contribute to their communities. One key message here was that it is impossible to pursue learning when basic needs are not being met, and that there is no point in pursuing technical and managerial skills if essential skills are lacking. There was strong consensus on the need to reduce barriers for individuals (for example, time and financial barriers, and fear of the learning system), and to reduce barriers and disincentives for employers (for example, tax burdens and the employment insurance system). The workshop on labour force issues for persons with disabilities stressed the need to eliminate economic disincentives to labour force participation, such as by separating disability support from social assistance. Other comments focussed on the need to build community capacity to support the inclusion of persons with disabilities, including bettering service delivery, supporting self-employment options, developing pre-employment skills, and establishing a clearinghouse to provide one-stop access to employability programs and services for persons with disabilities.

At HRDC's roundtable on children, participants stressed that social innovation should not be the "poor cousin" of economic innovation, saying that an inclusive society is a prerequisite for economic growth. Participants highlighted the need to address labour force issues that have a direct impact on the ability of parents and families to support their children's learning and development, such as the minimum wage, hours of work, and leave for family responsibilities. To really make a difference, participants called for attention to the conditions that enable healthy child development, including parents' time and family income.

Supporting the growth of clusters

The concept of developing clusters or innovation centres was generally supported, though many participants in the regional roundtables stressed that these need not be only in larger or urban centres. Virtual clusters captured as much, if not more, attention. Indeed, in some regions, the point was made that virtual clusters increase the likelihood of "have not" regional participation, particularly when they are supported by world-class interregional transportation and communications infrastructures, precisely because they aren't limited to one geographic locality. This view was also evident in submissions from individual citizens, who stressed that technology should be used to rise above geographic limitations. Some suggested that Canada should look at participating in trans-national clusters of innovation excellence, and several regional summits called for cluster support strategies. Ontario participants wanted sector-specific regional clusters that could be linked to R&D facilities. In British Columbia, participants suggested that rural growth clusters could be stimulated in areas of strength, for example, ocean technologies, forestry, fuel cells, life sciences and wireless telecommunications. In Nova Scotia, participants called on government to ensure that its own procurement encourages community and cluster development, and, in Newfoundland, participants suggested supporting the development of innovative clusters by establishing provincial advisory councils. In a number of Quebec summits, participants expressed strong support for organizing local structures into regional innovation networks.

In Northern Ontario, participants suggested establishing a regional private venture capital fund, and, elsewhere in the province, business leadership for skills development was seen as crucial to developing local innovative capacity. In Toronto, the lack of an innovation culture was cited as a major issue, and participants attributed it to complacency and an overreliance on the low Canadian dollar. In Ontario and the West, there were calls for municipalities to play a larger role in facilitating innovation at the local level; to put more emphasis on social innovation, which in Calgary was seen as crucial in bridging income gaps; and to address poverty and illiteracy.

Many participants in workshops and regional events raised the need for funding for communities to enable them to develop innovation strategies tailored to their unique circumstances. Participants also said that municipal, regional, provincial and federal bodies could work far more collaboratively and reduce duplication to promote efficient systems that help communities achieve their goals quickly. In this context, they suggested that there is a strong role for governments to play in sharing best practices across all sectors. They felt strongly that Canada's success in building innovative communities depends on the degree to which the cultural, social and geographical diversity of communities across this country is respected.

Finally, at many levels, regional participants stressed the need for branding and marketing efforts to attract talent and investments, and to raise awareness of the importance of innovation at the local level. As such, more people would be able to see the connection between innovation and their daily lives, and the contributions it makes to their quality of life.

> *"With focussed government support for innovation and learning, Canada will reap many benefits — such as desirable, high-paying jobs, increased tax revenue and economic benefits, and the development of entrepreneurial and highly skilled managerial cultures."*
>
> Peter Goodhand, President, MEDEC — Canada's Medical Devices Technology Companies

CHAPTER 3

WHAT WE HEARD FROM YOUNG CANADIANS

THE ENGAGEMENT PROCESS

A number of different engagement activities were undertaken in the summer of 2002 to gather the views of young Canadians for *Canada's Innovation Strategy*. HRDC hosted a roundtable discussion with 32 Canadians aged 16 to 29. Another 400 Canadians aged 20 to 32 participated in a series of 14 regional roundtables organized by Canada25, a not-for-profit, volunteer-based organization with a mandate to engage young Canadians in public policy debates. The Youth Action Council on Sustainable Innovation (YACSI) surveyed 241 high-achieving youth regarding their attitudes toward innovation. (YACSI works with youth between the ages of 2 and 25 to support the creation of an innovation culture.) The Alma Mater Society at the University of British Columbia brought together 50 students to engage in conversation about innovation, and the Saskatoon Chamber of

> **"*School prevents innovation. Some programs force [students] to repeat the same things — regurgitate information ... by teaching ... in a way that is too structured and does not allow students opportunities to think for themselves.*"**
>
> Youth Action Council for Sustainable Innovation Report

Commerce held a session with 13 of its members to discuss Canada's innovation challenges. Young Inventors International and the Youth Science Foundation Canada provided additional input through their own formal submissions.

The majority of input and feedback provided by young Canadians centred on skills, aligning the learning system with the labour market, and accessing the work force. However, young people also put forward suggestions in other areas of innovation performance, including R&D and commercialization, the regulatory and tax environment, and community capacity.

SKILLS AND LEARNING

Young people in all age groups were most concerned with issues of education and skills. Common to all groups were the need for mentorship in educational and workplace settings (along with internships and co-op/work programs), and a demand for more information to help them make better decisions about education and careers in all fields. They were also concerned about the state of the education system, and all advocated higher levels of public education funding. Older youth (age 24–32) focussed more of their critique on the post-secondary education system and on reforms to make the Canada Student Loans Program fairer and more equitable. Many felt that post-secondary institutions need to create innovative programs, and complained that course enrolments of 1000 or more are not conducive to learning.

They also wanted better relations with sector councils in order to better determine the skills needed for future employment opportunities; incentives for employers to invest in employee training; and high levels of investment in post-secondary institutions' basic operating budgets.

Specific issues raised by young people included:

- Financial responsibilities and increasing debt, which is deterring young Canadians from pursuing post-secondary education at a time when it is most important.

- Lack of exposure to a wide enough range of education and work opportunities. Participants felt that this range is necessary to ensure a well educated, diversely skilled labour force. Young Canadians said that, currently, advice is skewed to university and science/technology streams, and that young people need a much broader set of options to consider. They pointed out that exposure to the skilled trades is critically low, and that most young people don't know about these career opportunities unless they have a parent who works in the trades. Equally, they are not aware of available post-graduate opportunities.

- Insufficient counselling, coaching and mentorship in the post-secondary career planning process. Young people feel that their teachers and guidance counselors are stretched to the limit, at a time when navigating options in the post-secondary education system and modern workplace is more complex than ever.

- Insufficient levels of funding for Canada's education system. The view of young people is that, at present, funding levels are neither globally competitive nor commensurate with the importance placed on the education system to produce the resource most needed in a knowledge-based economy — skilled and knowledgeable people.

- Lack of encouragement for innovative, creative thinking in the current education system. Teachers focus on right and/or wrong solutions rather than problem-solving strategies and are too helpful, stifling students' ability to think for themselves.

- Opportunities to be involved in research are normally at graduate levels. More consideration should be given to supporting undergraduate research programs.

- Aboriginal youth expressed the view that in the North many youth do not see college or university as a goal because they are reluctant to leave their home communities and strong cultural environments to pursue post-secondary education elsewhere. More high quality e-learning opportunities would be welcome.

To address these challenges, young Canadians made a wide range of recommendations for action in three main areas: education access, skills and development, and workplace entry.

Education — Access to information and financing

Youth called for a more structured mentorship system that could be introduced to teenagers while still in high school. It would help students craft a set of education and work-related goals that could help them stay focussed so that, as they go on to higher learning, they feel they are learning with a purpose. The mentor would also be expected to expose the young person, through their personal and professional networks, to as many different work-related opportunities as possible. Roundtable participants in the 16 to 19 age group talked about career fairs where they could speak to people who work in a variety of different fields. They also suggested developing a data base of job profiles with biographies of people who hold those jobs, so that they can develop a better sense of career paths.

"We believe that the most important step the federal government could take in meeting the innovation challenge, and in successfully implementing its innovation strategy, would be the recognition of the paramount need for creating an innovation culture in Canada, particularly among Canadian teenagers."

Youth Science Foundation Canada

Participants also suggested establishing more degree-diploma "hybrid" post-secondary education programs, so that young people can learn how to "think" and how to "do" at the same time, obtain their degree and diploma in less time, and realize a better return on their investment in post-secondary education. One example would be the adoption of more work/study programs. They also called for improvements to distance education, but recognized that technology is only part of the access solution, and not necessarily an adequate substitute for being immersed in a learning community.

Young people also talked about the importance of encouraging "brain circulation" by providing more Canadian learners with access to international experiences and opportunities to study abroad. They also suggested there should be more interdisciplinary and multicultural educational opportunities, such as ones combining courses in engineering and business and taught by faculty in both departments, and by bringing national and global leaders into Canadian institutions.

Youth also suggested improving the communications infrastructure for Aboriginal communities and, more importantly, developing capabilities within the communities to sustain e-learning and distance education programs. Several institutions offer electronic curricula to let undergraduate students complete their education without ever setting foot in a classroom. Youth felt that, by building a strong network within these communities and educating their members about how to use the communications infrastructure to its full potential, more could be done to ensure Aboriginal youth have opportunities to participate in the knowledge economy without giving up their ways of life.

Finally, youth stressed the need to increase the basic operating budgets of colleges and universities to ensure adequate faculty, laboratories and libraries. In doing so, they suggested that faculties should begin to think more entrepreneurially and strive to be leaders in innovation. They also pointed to the need for more investments in infrastructure for colleges and continuing education programs, so that courses taken between institutions are more transferable.

Concerning the cost and debt barriers they face in accessing post-secondary education, a number of creative ideas were suggested, including:

- Instituting a "graduate tax" levy. Providing free post-secondary education for everyone. Graduates would pay a percentage of their base salary two years after they graduate for the following five years. All graduates would "feel" the repayment the same way because it would be calculated as a percentage of income, not as a flat fee.

- Offering a more flexible loan repayment system in the current Canada Student Loan Program that would provide more relief for students graduating with large debt loads.

- Creating an education mutual fund. Canadians would have the opportunity to invest in a fund to save for future education. Monies generated by the fund would be invested in student/ education/training-friendly firms committed to providing jobs, training and co-op experiences for youth.

Skills development

Young Canadians suggested that aligning skills development with the needs of the workplace should begin at the high school level, with life skills development courses and increased exposure to a wide variety of education and work-related opportunities, such as in skilled trades and in running their own businesses. However, young people also felt that skills training should be available for people of all ages, perhaps through the use of lifelong learning credits, which could be redeemed at participating institutions. They suggested that a lifelong learning credit system and/or deferred savings program could be particularly helpful in encouraging ongoing skills development among people without access to workplace-based training.

Participants also felt strongly that employers should be encouraged to provide training, through tax breaks and other incentives to pay for skills development and training. Such incentives could also offset the concerns businesses have about employees "learning and leaving." They felt that a managerial commitment among employers to support lifelong learning should be developed, and that this would support the development and supply of mentors. Finally, particularly for sectors of the economy where skills shortages are or will be a serious issue, young people suggested providing scholarships that could be designed in such a way as to ensure recipients remain in Canada (for example, by offering them the opportunity to work in world-class Canadian companies or in high-level public service positions). Youth also want programs, such as the Youth Employment Strategy, to emphasize innovation as a priority element, and to provide special assistance to groups working with young people so they can offer innovation-related services and programs.

Providing and promoting a "skills development and training" one-stop portal (Web site) was also suggested as a practical way to encourage access to skills development opportunities.

In addition, young Canadians recommended that skills targets in the *Innovation Strategy* be expanded to include:

- By 2012, ensure that every youth in Canada has basic innovation skills by the time they turn 25.

- By 2010, decrease the youth unemployment rate to the general unemployment rate.

- By 2007, double the yearly rate of businesses started by young people.

Workplace entry

Young people consistently stressed the importance of improving counselling, coaching and mentorship throughout the education and career planning process, to ensure that they have the guidance and networks they need to access meaningful work. They emphasized the need for a sustained commitment to expanding co-op programs and internships, so that more young people can be directly exposed to meaningful work opportunities and gain the practical work experience they need to contribute effectively to the labour market. The bottom line is that young people want faster entry into the work force for graduates, regardless of the level or type of education.

Immigration

Participating youth called for a number of measures to make Canada more attractive to immigrants, including young immigrants. They suggested offering graduates of any accredited university a one-year work permit to work in Canada, with options for renewal, to bring more young people to the country. They highlighted the need to develop international benchmarking programs to aid in the recognition of international universities and awarded degrees, as well as of immigrants' relevant skills. As well, youth called for professional associations or industry groups to produce prior learning assessments to gauge the skills and abilities of immigrants, so they can practice their professions or pursue further training in a timely fashion. They pointed to the need to establish standards for skills recognition. National professional associations, academic institutions and the government, they said, could all cooperate in establishing an international standard for skills, and a system for evaluating foreign credentials in relation to Canadian credentials (for example, by expanding programs such as the Academic Credential Assessment Service).

Youth also felt that more needs to be done to inform both current and prospective immigrants, as well as sector councils, about Canada's labour market; help ensure that people can check whether their credentials meet the requirements of industry before immigrating to Canada; and identify sectors where shortages of skilled workers are expected to contribute to input into international student recruitment and immigration policies.

In addition to their top innovation-related concerns on education, skills development, workplace entry, and immigration, certain groups of young Canadians provided their views on what could be done to improve Canada's R&D and commercialization outcomes, its innovation environment, and community capacity for innovation.

RESEARCH, DEVELOPMENT AND COMMERCIALIZATION

- Increase funding to the Natural Sciences and Engineering Research Council of Canada for youth innovation.

- Expand knowledge-performance targets to include broad-based contributions of non-R&D sectors.

- Invest in networks between industry, academia, government and other stakeholders to sustain innovative research and assist in its application and commercialization.

- Amend tax regulations to encourage private sector investment in the next generation of innovators and to encourage more small and medium-sized enterprises to undertake R&D.

- Increase access to venture capital.

- Conduct a public poll with young Canadians regarding ethical issues as they relate to innovation.

REGULATORY AND TAX ENVIRONMENT

- Develop services in addition to the Business Development Bank of Canada in order to expand access to venture capital (for example, by providing tax incentives to reward private investors who participate in venture initiatives).

- Consider accelerating the review of regulatory regimes, moving the deadline from 2010 to 2007.

- Streamline the regulatory environment to bring products/ideas to market faster.

- Take a holistic approach to developing an innovation culture that goes well beyond focussing on science and technology to all spheres of life and human endeavour.

STRENGTHENING COMMUNITIES

- Improve understanding of the relationship between innovation and economic development for smaller cities and communities, and of how clusters work.

- Extend broadband Internet access to all communities.

> **"We believe that Canadians must strive to be a community of creative thinkers, one where new ideas and approaches are held in the highest regard. We need to develop a culture . . . where we have a bias for risk and a healthy acceptance of failure, and a commitment to developing minds, not just skills."**
>
> Canada25

CHAPTER 4

WHAT WE HEARD FROM ABORIGINAL GROUPS

THE ENGAGEMENT PROCESS

A multifaceted approach was taken to solicit the views of Aboriginal groups and individuals on *Canada's Innovation Strategy*. Feedback from Aboriginal business was provided through Aboriginal Business Canada, an Industry Canada program that works with Aboriginal organizations to promote commerce as a means of self-sufficiency. Aboriginal Business Canada worked with the National Aboriginal Economic Development Board, the National Aboriginal Business Association and the National Aboriginal Capital Corporations Association, using the services of a professional facilitator. Additional submissions were received from the National Aboriginal Health Organization, the Nitawin Community Development Corporation, the Nunavut Library Association and the Council for the Advancement of Native Development Officers.

> **"It is our sincere hope that this initiative will constitute a real commitment to building partnerships with the Aboriginal community, and developing innovative responses to the economic and education challenges of Canada's Aboriginal population."**
>
> Council for the Advancement of Native Development Officers

As well, more than 550 Aboriginal individuals from across Canada were invited to participate in the regional innovation summits. Input was gathered from an HRDC-hosted national roundtable on Aboriginal skills and learning issues in Yellowknife in September 2002. There, experts and opinion leaders from across Canada, representing Aboriginal communities, businesses, labour, sector councils, governments and a range of learning institutions, presented their views.

The general view was that the *Innovation Strategy* needs a strong Aboriginal component with concrete solutions — a component that emphasizes flexible, community-based strategies, and that is based on dialogue and on improving the relationships between and among Aboriginal people, governments, industry, and labour. There was strong support at the skills and learning roundtable for a partnership approach to addressing Aboriginal skills and learning challenges. Without such an approach, participants felt Aboriginal people would be further marginalized as Canada evolves as a knowledge-based economy and society.

Stakeholders pointed to many basic quality of life issues confronting Aboriginal people, and made the case that addressing pressing social and economic issues, such as the need for housing and clean water, ultimately supports innovation. Many stakeholders suggested that, to start, the Government of Canada should revisit the 1996 report of the Royal Commission on Aboriginal Peoples and implement more of its recommendations.

SKILLS AND LEARNING

Skills development was the area that received the most attention from Aboriginal stakeholders. They identified education and training as key to participation in a knowledge-based economy. Participants repeatedly brought up the need to increase basic literacy skills and improve education for Aboriginal peoples of all ages, from school children to adults.

With respect to the Aboriginal adult work force, participants at the Aboriginal Skills and Learning Roundtable identified a number of areas requiring immediate attention. There was considerable discussion about emerging job opportunities in the natural resources sector. Many participants underscored the need for comprehensive training-to-employment plans to ensure that Aboriginal people can access these opportunities. It was suggested that plans should include the use of innovative methods such as prior learning assessments, workplace literacy programs and e-learning. In a similar vein, improvements in adult basic education systems and investments in Aboriginal post-secondary education were identified as essential to ensuring successful labour market participation for Aboriginal people. Participants also discussed apprenticeship issues at length. It was suggested that Aboriginal people should be positioned as a solution to Canada's skilled trades shortages. Participants stressed that labour union buy-in is essential to changing attitudes around issues, such as seniority, that may block access to apprenticeships and other skill development opportunities. Finally, stakeholders made the point that there should be more emphasis in the *Innovation Strategy* on educating Canadians, including developing Aboriginal adult and youth labour potential, before relying on attracting foreign students and training immigrants to address Canada's skill needs.

With respect to skills and learning issues for Aboriginal children and youth, participants at the Aboriginal Skills and Learning Roundtable called for:

- More funding for early childhood education, including funds for the continuation of Aboriginal Head Start programs;

- Standards for quality education for all children, and greater accountability for results;

- More direct investments in literacy and numeracy;

- The creation of teacher incentive programs;

- More mentorship programs, internships, and scholarships for post-secondary students;

- The provision of culturally-relevant career development decision-making tools;

- More support for Aboriginal post-secondary institutions;

- More culturally relevant post-secondary programs/curricula;

- Aboriginal awareness training for mainstream teachers;

- More distance education and off-campus education opportunities for Aboriginal people;

- Retention issues to be addressed early (that is, junior high); and

- Increased levels of post-secondary education funding for Aboriginal people.

"One hundred and ninety-five million dollars has been spent in Canada to develop public Internet access. LibraryNet recently reported the results of polls that show most southern Canadians associate public use computers with libraries. This illustrates the position libraries can have in the information infrastructure, but here in Nunavut many libraries cannot provide access to the Internet because their connection is either long distance dial-up and too costly, or too slow to be useful. In libraries that do have Internet access, staff have not had the necessary training to provide the value-added service of showing people how to use the Internet effectively. Libraries in Nunavut communities have the potential to be portals to the Web for a large segment of the community that cannot afford a computer."

Nunavut Library Association

STRENGTHENING COMMUNITIES

Stakeholders reinforced the importance of recognizing and accounting for regional differences and avoiding a top-down approach to innovation. Regarding their fundamental quality of life issues, stakeholders felt that, with the right support, Aboriginal communities have the capacity to find and apply innovative solutions, such as tele-health and distance learning. Part of providing better support involves removing the silos between and within federal, provincial and territorial governments that can act as barriers to Aboriginal efforts. However, most stakeholders emphasized that improved connectivity must not only establish links to universities and research centres, but literally connect rural and remote Aboriginal communities to the rest of Canada.

INNOVATION ENVIRONMENT

In the opinion of participating stakeholders, an improved environment for Aboriginal innovation would involve providing more economic development opportunities for Aboriginal people, including through federal procurement. In regards to regulations, Aboriginal stakeholders signaled that, in a knowledge-based economy, cultural property, including traditional Aboriginal knowledge, must be better protected. In addition, they emphasized the need to do more to market and advertise the federal programs available to support economic development and innovation, particularly programs for businesses.

On the human development side, participants in the Aboriginal Skills and Learning Round Table stressed the need for governments to streamline their processes, and develop systems that allow for partnerships and more coordinated efforts that minimize duplication and harness existing resources to achieve more powerful, focussed effects.

RESEARCH, DEVELOPMENT AND COMMERCIALIZATION

Aboriginal input concentrated on the definition of innovation being too focussed on science and technology. Given the basic needs in Aboriginal communities, particularly in education and skills, the emphasis on R&D and commercialization in the *Innovation Strategy* was seen as having limited direct potential benefit for Aboriginal people. Participants suggested expanding this area to include the application of knowledge for "useful innovations," along with undertaking a technological needs assessment for Aboriginal people.

> **"Recognizing that innovation occurs at the local level, governments must take a stewardship role rather than micro-management, and provide communities with the tools and policy environment to design, implement, and share their own solutions."**
>
> The Learning Enrichment Foundation

WHAT WE HEARD FROM BUSINESS ASSOCIATIONS, LABOUR AND ECONOMIC DEVELOPMENT ORGANIZATIONS, AND SECTOR COUNCILS

THE ENGAGEMENT PROCESS

As part of the engagement process, national business associations were invited to prepare formal responses to the *Innovation Strategy*. Submissions were received from national groups such as the Canadian Council of Chief Executives, the National Business Roundtable, the Canadian Chamber of Commerce, Canadian Manufacturers and Exporters, the Canadian Bankers Association, the Innovation Management Association of Canada and the Insurance Bureau of Canada. During the spring and summer of 2002, a number of community economic development organizations also submitted papers, including the Canadian Community Economic Development Network; the Ontario Association of Community Futures Development Corporations; and several groups operating at the municipal level, such as the Ottawa Centre for Research and Innovation; Smart Communities Demonstration Project Leaders; and Montréal TechnoVision. The Federation of Canadian Municipalities also responded, as did a small number of municipal governments.

Through roundtable events and conferences organized by HRDC, feedback was provided by major union and labour organizations, such as the United Steelworkers of America and the Canadian Labour Congress, and by sector councils,[1] who provided input to the *Innovation Strategy* through a day-long symposium, Partnerships that Work, that was convened by the Canadian Labour and Business Centre in conjunction with HRDC. Nearly 200 leaders from business, trade unions, sector councils and the education and training community took part in this event along with senior officials from federal and provincial governments. Representatives from sector councils, which provide services in such areas as skills accreditation and certification, e-learning, liaison with education/training organizations, labour market information, and occupational standards, also took part in other HRDC-sponsored events. HRDC received further comments through correspondence and bilateral meetings with groups such as the Ontario Society for Training and Development.

---

1. *Sector councils bring together employers, unions and other employee representatives with the education and training community to identify and respond to human resource challenges. They have become important players in the labour market and now operate in 26 industries (representing 25 percent of the work force), ranging from steel, mining and textiles to aerospace, construction and tourism.*

GENERAL IMPRESSIONS

National business associations largely endorsed the government's diagnosis of Canada's innovation challenge. As their top priorities, they saw an important federal role in creating a fertile environment for innovation through tax and regulatory reform, in supporting the skills and learning systems, and in encouraging collaboration among all players who influence the innovation system. Their submissions stressed the need for governments to reduce taxes, hold the line on spending, and bring down the debt-to-gross domestic product ratio. While viewing innovation as a collective responsibility, business associations believed that the private sector should direct investment to R&D and commercialization activities. They said that making improvements to the business and regulatory environment is the single most important element in a national strategy to create a culture of innovation, which in turn can permeate other areas of Canadian society. Their second priority was to invest in the education and skills of Canada's work force.

Economic development organizations concurred that the policy directions proposed in the *Innovation Strategy* papers are essentially sound. They welcomed the recognition of the community as an important forum for innovation, but pointed out that few municipalities have the financial or technical capacity to influence the pace of innovation on their own. They believed, however, that local authorities are well placed to deliver programs and services in conjunction with the senior levels of government, and stand ready to form the necessary networks and partnerships to play this role. One concern advanced by economic development organizations was that the *Innovation Strategy* is geared more toward large cities and overlooks the needs of smaller centres and rural areas, particularly in relation to learning facilities. The majority of recommendations from this group focussed on strengthening communities, local capacity building (for example, access to capital, broadband connectivity), and investments in human capital (for example, education and skills).

Sector council representatives who attended the "Partnerships that Work!" symposium were comfortable with the apprenticeship, workplace training, literacy and adult learning milestones set out in *Knowledge Matters*. What's more, they were confident that, with adequate support from government, sector councils would produce "measurable results that fully coincide with HRDC's priorities," while meeting the skills and learning needs of member-companies and their work force.

Throughout the engagement process, labour representatives repeated that building a skilled work force and strengthening the apprenticeship system are key priorities for Canada. Labour representatives were also concerned with the social dimensions of innovation, such as child care. In two best practice workshops, "Partnerships That Work!" and "Innovations in Workplace Skills and Learning," and the roundtable on "Building Community Capacity to Recognize Learning," labour representatives shared experiences of successful skills-enhancing initiatives.

REGULATORY AND TAX ENVIRONMENT

To improve Canada's innovation performance, national business associations placed comprehensive regulatory reform as their top priority. They called for a sector-by-sector review process to eliminate regulations that unduly impede business investment and operations. They also contended that the 2010 target date for regulatory review that is proposed in *Achieving Excellence* is too long, and believed the job could be completed by 2005.

Business associations strongly believe that a healthy fiscal environment is the most critical public policy element in the *Innovation Strategy*. They called for continuous program review to generate savings within federal departments to support lower personal and corporate taxes. They held that these measures will attract international investment and highly skilled people, and will result in increased productivity gains. Business associations stressed that Canadian business and personal tax levels must be more competitive with other industrialized countries, and that international comparisons should fully reflect the impact of government user fees. They were particularly concerned over the burden of capital taxes, which, they believed, significantly impairs Canada's innovation performance.

Economic development organizations concurred regarding the need to eliminate capital taxes and proposed other measures to stimulate innovation, including a tax credit program aimed specifically at investments in new start-up companies. They pointed out that federal and provincial investments in core municipal infrastructure, including transit systems, can have a positive impact on the innovation environment by helping communities attract investment and skilled workers. They also recommended that government showcase innovative practices in their own operations and lead by example, particularly in providing on-line services to citizens. They called on federal, provincial and municipal authorities to collaborate in establishing national standards for connectivity and e-government.

Several national business associations stated that actions on climate change, including ratification of the Kyoto Protocol, could change the regulatory burden on Canadian industry and could potentially impact progress on innovation. On the other hand, economic development organizations pointed out that federal investments in municipal transit systems and reuse and recycling facilities could have a positive impact on greenhouse gas emissions. According to this group, this type of support for municipalities could form part of Canada's climate change response and also encourage innovation at the community level.

Aligning the learning system to reflect labour market needs

National business associations place enormous priority on human capital and view the skills and knowledge capacity of the work force as critical drivers of innovation. They urged the government to show leadership on this front by investing more in the learning system and by encouraging the multistakeholder collaboration necessary to build a world-class work force. Associations stressed that targets in areas such as post-secondary graduation or participation rates in adult education are irrelevant if the collaborative education framework and education–industry partnerships needed to achieve them are not in place.

Business associations endorsed the *Innovation Strategy* objective of increasing the number of master's and PhD enrolments by 5 percent annually. They emphasized, however, that Canada's skills challenge goes well beyond increasing the supply of post-secondary graduates and highly skilled people. Several submissions touched on the need to invest more in the K-12 education system, to put greater emphasis on business and management skills in the high school curriculum, and to give young people more sophisticated career information and counselling to support wise learning choices. They also called for greater attention to literacy and numeracy problems, adult education, better apprenticeship training, and workplace training and measures to improve employability skills for Aboriginal Canadians. Improving labour force mobility through greater portability of credentials across provincial boundaries, along with better recognition of the skills of immigrants, was also seen as a key factor in developing the Canadian talent pool.

Economic development organizations raised many of the same points and also stressed the need to make learning opportunities more accessible to Canadians in rural and remote communities. They expressed an urgent need to create locally available training opportunities for entrepreneurship and apprenticeship, as well as to address the ongoing migration of youth from rural areas.

Community organizations underscored that prior learning assessments and recognition are necessary components in labour force development given the proven value in recognizing knowledge and skills, promoting transferability, saving time and money in education, and creating individual confidence. They added that matching community needs assessments with prior learning assessments for individuals helps to sustain more meaningful attachments to the labour force over the long term.

Sector councils stressed the point that there is more to meeting the "skills challenge" than producing scientists and engineers. They shared the concerns expressed by business associations and economic development organizations over the shortage of skilled tradespeople, which will soon pose a significant barrier to innovation and growth in Canada. They were confident, however, that sector councils could alleviate this situation by spearheading efforts to address the "image problem" of the skilled trades and actively marketing trades careers to students in the K-12 system as well as to teachers, guidance counselors and parents. In addition, sector councils are strongly interested in advancing Canada's apprenticeship system in ways that make it more responsive to industry requirements and appealing to young people. They are prepared to play a significant role in improving the quality, and expanding the value, of employer-sponsored skills development, as well as in developing and sharing training infrastructure, such as distance learning facilities, and are well placed to contribute to the development of more accurate, timely and user-friendly labour market information systems in Canada.

A further thought was that sector councils could partner with the Aboriginal Human Resources Development Council of Canada to help Aboriginal youth enter the labour force, particularly in the construction trades.

Labour organizations suggested that businesses and governments need to better respond to workers' expectations and priorities in training, and that a worker-centred agenda for training needs to be more broadly based rather than merely "machine-specific." At the roundtable on Building Community Capactiy to Recognize Learning, organized labour called for greater business and government investment in training for employees, particularly considering that when compared to other countries, Canada leads in terms of employees paying for their own training. Organized labour saw its role as continuing to put pressure on businesses to invest in employee skills development, and said that they are eager to be part of the solution in the workplace.

On the apprenticeship issue, labour representatives acknowledged that more Canadians must be encouraged to become apprentices and to remain in the skilled trades, which they considered a vital link in meeting the demand for a skilled work force in all parts of the economy. They agreed that this will involve overcoming the negative images that trades have, and enhancing support for apprentices, journeypersons and employers in the apprenticeship system.

At the "Partnerships that Work!" event, a representative of the United Steelworkers of America explained that both unions and management must deal with tough issues such as restructuring, new technology and skills gaps, but each from their own perspectives. Sector councils were applauded for providing a forum where unions and management can work together to meet their respective and collective needs. They enable unions to identify skill requirements and develop training programs that help union members. This, in turn, leads to skills upgrading in the current work force, which benefits the employer. This type of "win–win" outcome was identified from essential skills development programs at the "Innovations in Workplace Skills and Learning" workshop. A representative from the Canadian Labour Congress explained how essential skills positively affect workers' lives and, in turn, positively affect organizations and businesses by creating safer, more empowered, and productive workplaces.

Like many others who participated in the *Innovation Strategy* consultations, labour representatives said there is a need for more innovative social policies and programs that promote inclusion. They pointed out that many parents are disadvantaged in the labour force (for example, by the time crunch and resulting stress for low-income parents, many of whom must hold a number of jobs in order to earn an adequate income) and, as a result, are unable to access skills upgrading programs. They stressed that efforts to build a skilled work force must be matched with efforts to strengthen the services available to workers and families. In addition, they argued that adequate income and supports for working parents are needed to ensure healthy development and early learning. They added that services and income are intertwined, saying that, without supports like child care, parents cannot earn an adequate income. Labour representatives called for more inclusive approaches to child care (that is, making it available to all, regardless of income) and for the regeneration of labour standards that include hours of work and minimum-wage-related issues.

Immigration

Business associations believed that modernizing Canada's immigration system will be key to assuring that Canada attracts its fair share of the world's mobile talent. "Partnerships that Work!" participants arrived at a similar consensus, and sector councils believed they could play a more active role in the immigration process, particularly in providing prior learning assessment and recognition services to potential immigrants and new arrivals.

STRENGTHENING COMMUNITIES

Broadband

Leaders from economic development organizations strongly endorsed accelerated funding of the broadband initiatives discussed in *Achieving Excellence*. They believed that broadband access creates major economic spinoffs, attracts research investments and enables innovation in the development of content and applications. Economic development organizations saw nationwide broadband infrastructure and affordable Internet access as key to addressing the "urban–rural digital divide" and to ensuring that the opportunities of the knowledge-based economy extend to all regions. They also stressed that governments must show exemplary leadership in putting broadband facilities to work in areas such as telehealth, e-learning and e-democracy, and in enhancing the visibility and accessibility of government services.

New partnerships

Leaders from economic development organizations called for a new kind of partnership that would marry the superior financial resources and broad strategic perspective of the federal government with the intimate understanding of local conditions enjoyed by economic development authorities at the municipal level. They believed that this dovetailing of national and local capacity would lead to better programs and services, particularly for small and medium-sized enterprises in the start-up phases. Another idea was for the Government of Canada to work with cities or organizations such as the Federation of Canadian Municipalities to identify and address human resource and other capacity gaps at the municipal level. This would assist communities in developing and implementing innovation strategies that would complement federal and provincial measures. Proposals from the Federation of Canadian Municipalities reinforced their willingness to participate in overcoming human resource capacity gaps and investing in community innovation plans.

Clusters

Economic development organizations view industry clusters as critically important for incubating new business start-ups, and encouraging R&D and the follow-through to commercialization. They also believe that governments can encourage the formation of clusters by investing in local research and learning facilities and strategically locating their own research and scientific activities to attract a critical mass of highly qualified personnel, skilled workers, and investors. While viewing support from senior levels of government as essential, they made clear at the same time that the creation of new industry clusters must be a "bottom-up process," driven by community leaders.

They also cautioned that government efforts to support the creation of new industry clusters should not come at the expense of existing clusters. They suggested that the target proposed in *Achieving Excellence* of creating 10 internationally recognized technology clusters by 2010 was arbitrarily conceived and may end up spreading scarce human and capital resources too thinly across the country.

RESEARCH, DEVELOPMENT AND COMMERCIALIZATION

Business associations called for a wholesale rethinking of government programs that encourage venture capital formation and, in turn, support R&D and commercialization. They believed that many of these programs have changed little in a decade, while the relevant capital, product and labour markets have evolved considerably. To support private sector innovation, they strongly preferred a shift to tax-based incentives over new program spending. Indeed, one association called for a "zero-base" review to eliminate business subsidies that do not encourage innovative behaviour. They were confident that tax-based strategies could stimulate the supply of venture capital and encourage angel investors to support promising companies during the difficult start-up phase. Associations also urged the government to move quickly toward a review of Canada's intellectual property laws.

Economic development organizations strongly supported a concerted, national effort to boost investment in R&D. However, some questioned the feasibility of the objective to have Canada rank within the top five R&D countries in the world by 2010. They also stressed that R&D targets should not be seen as an end unto themselves. They viewed R&D as a critical input to innovation, but thought that the outputs — ideas that make it to the marketplace — are what really count and are more worth measuring.

> **" The Innovation Strategy is an opportunity for communities to voice their own opinions and share their own innovative solutions."**
>
> The Learning Enrichment Foundation

Economic development organization representatives believed that federal R&D support programs should also offer explicit follow-through incentives to encourage firms to commercialize their research findings. They called for broader eligibility criteria under the Industrial Research Assistance Program to extend support to community development organizations that facilitate the flow of capital from investors to small and medium-sized enterprises.

Business associations called for new measures to stimulate investment in commercialization of research. However, they also saw a strong skills element to the commercialization challenge and highlighted the need to expand Canada's cadre of innovation managers through mentorship and other targeted training programs.

CHAPTER 6

WHAT WE HEARD FROM INDUSTRY SECTORS

This chapter is divided into two parts. Part A presents the views of a wide range of industry sectors, but excludes the information and communication technology sector. Views expressed by information and communication technology stakeholders are treated separately in Part B.

A: VIEWS FROM CANADIAN INDUSTRIES

THE ENGAGEMENT PROCESS

This section brings together the views, ideas and concerns of leaders from a wide range of participating sectors, ranging from traditional manufacturers and processors, such as construction, aluminum and textiles, to new industries, such as environmental sciences and bio-products, to cultural industries, such as those engaged in creating and disseminating information and cultural products. The federal government often initiated these engagement activities and relied on industry "champions" to assemble input from their stakeholders. Champions submitted final reports and often met with government officials to discuss their findings.

"Government cannot create innovation. Once it removes barriers, it will be up to individuals and organizations to create innovations."

Aluminium Association of Canada

HRDC best practices events and expert roundtables also provided venues for the private sector, labour, non-governmental organizations, and learning and community organizations to discuss skills and learning issues, concerns, suggestions, best practices and recommendations affecting the industry sector.

GENERAL IMPRESSIONS

For the most part, industry sectors responded favourably to the government's diagnosis of Canada's innovation challenges. Industry leaders accepted the need for national sectoral strategies to integrate the goals and activities of all stakeholders. They suggested, however, that the *Achieving Excellence* document places too much emphasis on the new economy and fails to appreciate the enormous potential of Canada's traditional industries to bring new products and production processes on stream. Similarly, some thought there was too much emphasis on manufacturing and processing industries, while the productivity-enhancing contribution of innovation in transportation and other service activities was understated. Another general concern was that the document focusses too narrowly on "economic growth and prosperity" while overlooking the contribution innovation can make in the areas of sustainable development and environmental protection.

Most industry leaders acknowledged that the private sector has a leading role in forging a culture of innovation. At the same time, they viewed their role as part of a collective responsibility in which governments, the education and research communities, trade unions, professional organizations, the voluntary sector, and other groups all have a role to play.

Industry leaders also believe that the key innovation challenges go far beyond economic variables and are rooted in stimulating creative thought and expression and changing the Canadian mindset about risk, reward and success. Some industry sectors called on governments to play a leadership role in developing a long-term vision that spans political regimes and provides a coherent strategy for disparate industry sectors. They also made it clear that investment counts. As one industry group pointed out, moving Canada from 15th place to among the top five in the world in R&D investment spending by 2010 will require spending an additional $26 billion per year. Another industry group suggested that it will take an additional $250 billion in annual sales, mostly in export markets, to support this level of investment.

Industry reaction to the government's specific policy directions was largely positive. Leaders applauded, for example, the emphasis on regulatory reform, although most believed that the proposed 10-year time frame for regulatory review should be reduced to five years. They were also unanimous in recognizing the explicit connection between innovation and a highly skilled work force. Many, however, cautioned that the need for advanced scientific and technical skills should not overshadow an equally important requirement for managerial talent and skilled tradespeople.

With respect to the goal of strengthening innovation capacity at the community level, there was a greater range of opinions. Most industry reports recognized that communities with a knowledge infrastructure and a critical mass of entrepreneurs and investors will become magnets for innovation. However, several argued against active top-down policies to establish technology clusters, suggesting instead that in a positive regulatory and taxation environment clusters will emerge on their own around the innovation strengths and capacities of particular locales. Most agreed that government has a partnering role in support of already emerging clusters.

> **"The high cost of capital in Canada, which is in part a function of the regulation and taxation systems, is the largest single barrier to increased investment in technology, human resources and R&D."**
>
> Canadian Electricity Association

One very encouraging thread running through this conversation with Canadian industry leaders was the clear belief that new and stronger partnerships among individual firms, between government and industry, and between industry and the education and training community, are critical to the success of the innovation initiative. Indeed, the fact that emerging sectors dominated by small firms, such as the languages industry or the renewable energy sector, came together to contribute to the *Innovation Strategy* underscores the private sector's willingness to explore new kinds of partnerships with the government. Particular views of industry sector groups regarding R&D and commercialization, skills, innovation environment and strengthening communities are outlined in the next section.

RESEARCH, DEVELOPMENT AND COMMERCIALIZATION

Sector leaders strongly believed that expanding our capacity to create knowledge through pure and applied research is a key building block for a more innovative Canada. They unanimously endorsed the increased funding for granting councils and university-based research announced in the Government of Canada's 2001 budget. At the same time, several submissions called on funding agencies to be more open to "curiosity-based research" that would allow scientists to pursue promising "hunches" that may break new theoretical ground and lead to innovation further down the road.

Industry leaders clearly believe that government can and should do more to stimulate R&D through a more flexible and generous tax credit regime, strategic procurement policies, and by reinforcing the science and research capacities of federal departments. There was also a call for new partnerships that would allow government, industry and universities to share both research facilities and scientific, technical and management personnel. Some also saw a need for government to articulate the roles of universities, governments and private industry within a national R&D framework to achieve a more productive mix of basic and applied research. Universities and government should focus more on basic research and industry applications. A long-term research agenda (20 to 50 years) is key, and needs to be advanced by government, because that time scale reaches beyond the commercial interests of corporations.

Resource-based sectors supported the position that R&D should be recognized as a long-term game that requires collaboration, and that Canada should focus its R&D and commercialization policies in areas where there is the greatest potential for Canadian advantage, such as the resource sector.

Across the board, Canada's industry sectors agreed that, to bring R&D investments to world-class levels, government and the private sector will have to spend more and spend smarter. For example, some called for a national mechanism to be put in place to set R&D priorities in areas such as municipal infrastructure, health, housing and sustainable development. Others talked about coordinating non-proprietary research on an industry-by-industry basis and creating an accessible Canadian R&D data base to reduce costly duplication and overlap. Another suggestion was to channel tax-financed R&D spending primarily to researchers with strong and established track records. While each industry sector had its own specific ideas, all agreed on the need for a more strategically planned approach to R&D spending in Canada and/or changes to the scientific research and experimental development tax credit program. Many also concurred that international R&D partnerships are an important stimulus for innovation in Canadian industry.

Commercialization

Industries argued that there is a technology commercialization gap in many sectors, from oil and gas to bio-products.

Sector leaders felt that government should help companies develop new products and processes by shouldering more of the risks. Noting that "too much good R&D gets left on the shelf," industry champions urged policy makers to inject a "from concept to market" approach into commercialization programs, as is done, for example, in federal energy, science and technology. While the corporate share of investment should increase as the R&D moves closer to commercialization, government has a critical role in regulation and taxation regimes to enable the private sector to succeed. It also has a role to play as a catalyst in undertaking long-term, high-risk R&D.

Another key message was that improved access to venture capital and high-risk export financing is vitally important to boosting the pace of innovation in Canadian firms. Some thought that changes to the Business Development Bank of Canada such as a more explicit commercialization mandate would be helpful. Another idea was to follow the lead of other G-8 countries and create a Canadian development finance institution. Others felt that better cooperation among existing institutions, including the Business Development Bank of Canada, Export Development Canada and the chartered banks, would improve the supply of flexible, long-term financing. Further suggestions included relaxing restrictions on early-stage initial public offerings and offering tax incentives to suppliers of "patient capital" to improve the flow of capital to small and medium-sized enterprises.

Most submissions from the manufacturing, processing and energy sectors called for more funding to successful initiatives such as the Canada Foundation for Innovation, as well as Industrial Research Assistance Program, the Program of Energy Research and Development, Technology Early Action Measures, and Technology Partnerships Canada. A number also wanted government to clarify cost-recovery policies, broaden the mandates and eligibility criteria for the aforementioned programs, and simplify application procedures to facilitate more access for small and medium-sized enterprises.

Several sectors also suggested that government could use its procurement policies to encourage commercialization by supporting demonstration projects that involve new technology, and through Canadian content regulations for large-scale capital projects.

"Speed to market is a critical ingredient of success in today's fast-paced world, particularly for small high-tech companies whose only real asset is their usually unproven intellectual property. What is required is an innovative financing regime that can support a balanced and simultaneous approach to both product development and market development."

Canadian Centre for Marine Communications

INNOVATION ENVIRONMENT

Industry leaders emphasized that greater clarity, stability, certainty and coherence in federal, provincial and municipal policies, programs, and regulations would have a positive impact on private-sector investment, which, in turn, would promote R&D and commercialization. There was a strong sense that tax and regulatory measures, intellectual property laws, and competition and trade policy should all be seen as potential levers for stimulating innovation.

Solid public commercial infrastructure, including widely accessible, high-speed broadband and a first-rate public education system were also widely seen as innovation environment factors.

Regulatory reform

For industry leaders, particularly in the biotechnology, natural resources (energy, minerals and metals, forestry), environmental, pharmaceutical and medical devices sectors, regulatory reform is a top priority. Participants widely endorsed the need to reduce red tape and speed up certification processes. They argued for a simplification and harmonization of regulation and a regulatory framework that would improve productivity and competitiveness, as well as Canada's position relative to the U.S. Many spoke of an urgent need to harmonize product acceptance codes and other standards among the provinces and, through negotiations, with our major trading partners.

A number of submissions stated that industry sectors accept the need for regulation, but expressed concern that, in many instances, the regulatory machinery slows the ability of Canadian firms to respond to global market opportunities. These participants suggested that a comprehensive, sector-by-sector regulatory review could be completed by 2005, well ahead of the 10-year deadline proposed in *Achieving Excellence*. Another frequent comment was that government itself must strive to innovate by developing "modern" regulatory processes that balance health, safety, environmental and other concerns with the competitive realities facing innovative firms.

Several industry sectors stated that actions on climate change could impose new regulatory burdens and make Canada less attractive to R&D investors. Others had different views. Submissions from the energy sector, for example, stressed that the *Innovation Strategy* must embrace the goal of mitigating climate change and lowering greenhouse gas emissions. They saw innovation as key to achieving this objective.

On the regulatory front, cultural industries had unique concerns relating to Canadian content rules in broadcasting and protecting intellectual property rights for artists, performers, writers, and other creative talents; the biotechnology and pharmaceutical sectors were concerned about lengthy patent approval processes; and the forestry, mining, and oil and gas sector leaders called for greater use of performance-based environmental regulation, and greater attention to Aboriginal entitlements in order to provide "certain and predictable" access to land and resources.

Tax measures

Every sector submission commented on Canada's tax regime and its impact on corporate investment decisions. While applauding recent steps to reduce the federal tax burden, industry leaders cautioned that more needs to be done to create a "visible tax advantage" to encourage Canadian firms and multinational corporations operating in Canada to invest in product and process innovations. Most said that, compared to our competitors, tax rates on corporate profits and personal incomes are still too high, and that the federal and provincial governments must move quickly to harmonize tax policies. Many believed capital taxes, which are not tied to performance or profitability, are extremely detrimental to innovation and should be eliminated altogether. There was also a prevalent view that a substantial reduction in Employment Insurance premiums would free up capital for investing in innovation, especially among small and medium-sized enterprises.

Most of these submissions discussed the impact of scientific research and experimental development tax credits, and offered ideas for improving their effectiveness. Some suggested extending the range of eligible expenditures to include such things as market research and other non-laboratory-based activities, and, where no Canadian capacity exists, to work performed outside of Canada. Others called for longer carry-forward periods, an increase in the current $2-million expenditures cap, and an investigation into the merits of letting firms sell their tax credits as a source of financing.

A number of industry leaders believe that the R&D tax credit program is not "small business-friendly," and that cumbersome application processes pose a real barrier to "microfirms." It was suggested that the Canada Customs and Revenue Agency could work with industry on an education program that would show small firms how R&D activities might qualify for tax relief.

Several submissions emphasized that Canada's R&D incentives compete head to head with those offered in other countries, and, particularly, by U.S. state governments. A related point was that Canada's tax incentives must be aggressive enough to overcome the bias of multinational corporations towards doing their R&D work in their home countries.

Market development

Sector leaders agreed that improving our innovation environment is key to "branding" Canada as a producer of high-quality products and services, and a good place to work and invest. One suggestion was for government and industry to adopt a "Team Canada" approach, highlighting Canada's success stories and marketing our brand to the world.

In addition to addressing the question of "image," some leaders called for a concerted effort to put home-grown technology to wider use, instead of importing the bulk of our knowledge-based products. Some submissions also called for a Canadian strategy to attract international research projects. This, they said, would give Canada's research specialists the opportunity to work with experts from around the world and to develop skills that would spill over into other R&D projects. At the same time, these participants thought that international projects might help repatriate Canadian scientists working abroad, and attract foreign scientists to Canada.

SKILLED WORK FORCE

Industry leaders see an intimate connection between innovation performance and a highly skilled work force, and most called for governments to increase public spending on K-12 and post-secondary education. As one submission put it: "We need a harmonized, cooperative approach to education, with a single cohesive vision" to build a world-class work force. Many submissions acknowledged the work force demographic issues that are looming large for Canada, and considered adult education and lifelong learning to be key pillars of any work force development strategy.

One point that came up repeatedly was that Canada's human resource challenge must be seen in broader terms than ensuring the supply of scientists, engineers and technicians. In many sectors, the most urgent requirement is for skilled tradespeople and highly adaptable "practitioners." As one submission put it, this requirement "will not be met [solely] by increasing the supply of university graduates." Others suggested that, in relation to master's degree and PhD holders, the problem is not so much one of shortages but of absorbing these highly qualified people into the work force. This "integration" challenge was seen as a particular problem for small firms.

> "*We must establish a system that will reliably identify, support and reward genuine innovators — or someone else will.*"
>
> Canadian Association of Petroleum Producers

Aligning the learning system to reflect labour market needs

A key priority for industries is to reinforce linkages between their sectors, government and the education community. These linkages are necessary to ensure that curricula, teachers and students stay in touch with constantly changing skill requirements and labour market conditions.

"Producing more science graduates is one of the main hurdles Canada needs to overcome to fuel innovation in the biotechnology sector. Success in achieving this priority will depend on the ability of government and industry to partner on the common goal of encouraging students to study science."

Aventis Pasteur

A number of industry sectors suggested that K-12 and post-secondary schools should shift away from applied technology and higher-order skills, and towards basic science, creative thinking and management skills. Many felt that the foundations for a more innovative culture can be laid in primary and secondary schools that recognize and reward creativity, stimulate the entrepreneurial spirit, and expose young learners to real-life work situations and problems through high-quality co-op, internship and related programs. Leaders in the cultural industries urged policy makers to acknowledge the role that culture plays in engaging young people in learning. As one pointed out, "There is more to learning than improving math and science scores." They added that talents that are critical for innovation, such as creativity, initiative, patience, flexibility and pride, are all developed through participation in the arts. At the post-secondary level, there was a call to address skills gaps in innovation management and financing by coupling business schools with science and engineering faculties, and building management, marketing, and communications elements into science and engineering programs. Certain sectors lamented that continuing education in the form of readily accessible adult training for those already in the labour force lags considerably behind that of competitors in the United States, Britain, Denmark, Sweden and Finland. They recommended that closer linkages be formed between universities and colleges, industry, and governments to identify skill requirements and to ensure that effective strategies are put into place. They also suggested that much more needs to be done to help new graduates overcome the job experience hurdle, for example through first-job internships. Participants felt this would help companies in their quest for instantly productive, experienced workers.

Leaders from a wide range of sectors also made it clear that it is time for Canada to get serious about the looming shortage of skilled tradespeople. They said there is an urgent need for a marketing program to address the "image problem" of the skilled trades and to ensure that students in the K-12 system understand the opportunities that the trades offer (for example, in transportation services). They also called on governments, industry, trade unions and educators to collaborate in developing new, innovative approaches to apprenticeship programs that will appeal to young people. Stronger partnerships with colleges and universities are needed to develop co-op programs, work terms and apprenticeships in a much broader range of industry sectors.[1]

At the "Apprenticeship is the Future" HRDC workshop, the focus of many of the presentations and discussions was on how to encourage more Canadians to consider skilled trades as a career choice, and on how to encourage them to remain in the skilled trades. Issues ranged from overcoming the negative image trades have to the need for enhanced support for apprentices/journeypersons and employers in the apprenticeship system. Participants felt that prior learning assessments and recognition continue to play important roles in apprenticeship training by allowing workers to accelerate their training.

---

1. *It was noted that about 50 percent of Canadian apprentices are employed in one sector — the construction industries. More industries would like to participate in apprenticeship programs.*

Delegates said there is a need to share more information within and across sectors, including up-to-date labour market information and forecasting. They also underscored the considerable scope of increasing participation and ensuring access to apprenticeship for underrepresented groups. This point was picked up at the workshop on a labour market strategy for persons with disabilities, where participants suggested increasing business and labour awareness of disability issues, including by working with employers and unions to address barriers and the myths of accommodation. Delegates also called for adequate research on persons with disabilities, including qualitative research and documentation of best practices in areas such as flexible alternative work arrangements.

At the HRDC roundtable on the adult labour force, there was also widespread agreement on the need to increase the number of apprentices and overcome the image problem of the skilled trades. Participants pointed to the need for a marketing strategy to promote adult learning, and for actions to reduce barriers for individuals (for example, barriers of time, finances and fear of learning system) and barriers and disincentives for employers. There was strong support for a sector council role in this regard, particularly since sector councils provide a mechanism by which to deliver economies of scale to small and medium-sized enterprises, and to share information and best practices on recruitment, training, adjustment and other human resource challenges, across a wide range of industries. Participants called on HRDC to increase core funding and better exploit the potential of sector councils.

Delegates at the HRDC roundtable on building community capacity to recognize learning also agreed that a national system for recognizing workplace learning is necessary and should be supported by all stakeholders. They suggested that this system will require the commitment and leadership of government, industry, sector councils, labour organizations and education institutions.

Training

There was a strong sense that Canadian industry can do more to bring its training efforts up to par with the United States, the United Kingdom, and other countries. There was a broad and strong belief, however, that in order to achieve this, governments must underwrite a larger share of the costs, whether through direct contributions, by supporting sector councils, or through a training tax credit system.

Leaders in several sectors believed that some kind of mechanism connecting young entrepreneurs and managers, particularly in small and medium-sized enterprises, with mentors in other organizations would help develop much-needed management and leadership skills.

At HRDC's "Innovations in Workplace Skills and Learning" workshop, participants discussed two specific workplace training issues: essential skills and recognizing workplace learning. Essential skills training provides the foundation skills that workers need to learn technical and managerial skills. Participants suggested that sector councils were an effective mechanism for delivering essential skills programming, and recommended that support be provided for workplace and career development practitioners who develop and implement this training.

With respect to recognizing workplace learning, workshop participants stressed the importance of prior learning assessment and recognition as a key component in labour force development. They said prior learning assessment and recognition has proven its value in recognizing knowledge and skills, promoting transferability, saving time and money in education, and increasing individuals' confidence. All delegates expressed a need for greater access to information about recognition of workplace learning, including both program models and existing research. They emphasized that this would also help promote awareness and recognition of adult learning needs. The workshop's small enterprises and sector councils group added that there is a need to include identification of specific industry needs within a larger, pan-Canadian system of workplace learning recognition, in order to accommodate specific industry priorities.

They suggested that sector councils could play a leading role in ensuring that small businesses are consulted in this process.

> **"We will work with the federal government to ensure the innovation strategy is in line with regional needs and be its partner for implementation in the Ottawa region."**
>
> Ottawa Centre for Research and Innovation

At the HRDC roundtable on building community capacity to recognize learning, participants argued that the assessment and recognition of prior learning is a necessary component in labour force growth, creating opportunities to integrate marginalized Canadians as well as immigrants. Participants stressed the need for a cohesive process in assessing the prior learning of immigrants (that is, skills acquired through experience in their home countries), which participants stressed is a different and more comprehensive issue than foreign credential recognition alone. Participants identified using prior learning assessment and recognition to help fill shortages in skilled trades as a useful way to integrate workers who have been certified in other provinces or countries. Recommended actions included developing empirical data to determine how recognizing learning contributes to social and economic growth.

Immigration

Sector leaders agreed on the vital importance of immigration in meeting their human resource needs. In general, industry sector reports reinforced the need for a skills-based immigration policy, and, in particular, for changes to the points system that would reward demonstrated skills as much as educational background. They also recommended a more flexible Temporary Foreign Worker Program, fast-track procedures for bringing highly qualified people to Canada,

and a more strategic approach to attracting top-flight foreign students and encouraging them to stay in Canada after graduation.

Most industry leaders stated that employers should play a more active role in the immigrant selection and recruitment process, and that industry should work with governments to establish certification standards that would speed up the integration of foreign-trained professionals and skilled workers into the labour force. However, they cautioned that immigration should not be seen as a substitute for improving Canada's education and training systems, or for programs to develop the country's domestic work force.

STRENGTHENING COMMUNITIES

A number of submissions presented the view that economic, industrial and community development go hand in hand and will require new partnerships linking industry to the education and training communities, and to the various levels of government. Several suggested, for instance, that federal support for physical and social infrastructure that has a direct bearing on quality of life will be increasingly important in attracting the skilled workers and highly qualified people who drive innovation to Canadian cities. Similarly, in the land-based resource industries, leaders noted that, to secure support in local communities, companies are being required to demonstrate "a clearer and more determined sense of corporate social responsibility and new innovative partnerships."

Industry clusters

Most sector submissions argued that communities that are able to attract a critical mass of entrepreneurs and investors can become hubs for innovation and can provide the foundations for mutually beneficial province-to-province or country-to-country R&D relationships. Some believed that governments should actively support the development of industry clusters through tax and program measures and by using other levers, such as locating government laboratories and academic institutions together in order to capitalize on the benefits and synergies of geography.

Others noted that, in some sectors, physical co-location is not important and that a "virtual cluster model" may make more sense. Still, they believed that government support for clusters should have a place in a national vision for innovation. There were several proposals for cluster support, including fuel cells, energy efficiency, ocean technologies, language industries, bioproducts, cleaner hydrocarbons, an international marine cluster, forest products and others. An example of a sector that lends itself to the virtual model is industrial energy efficiency. A positive policy framework to support clusters and an examination of how competitors promote clusters was called for.

Another school of thought was that clusters happen — they are not made. Many industry leaders believed that clusters form and grow based on local strengths and advantages, as long as governments create the right macroeconomic conditions through tax, education, infrastructure, procurement and other policy levers. Several submissions questioned the 10-technology cluster target proposed in *Achieving Excellence*. Others were cautiously supportive, but warned of potential pitfalls, such as duplication of facilities spreading scarce capital and human resources too thinly.

Broadband

There was very strong support among industry leaders for the Government of Canada's efforts to build broadband infrastructure in all regions of Canada. They saw this as an essential factor in strengthening communities and offering a solid advantage to Canadian firms trying to penetrate global markets.

" The development and application of enabling technologies should be a major focus of Canada's Innovation Strategy. These technologies, such as intelligent systems, broadband networks, microelectronics, biotechnology and nanotechnology, radiate benefits throughout the economy and provide the underpinnings of many industrial sectors."

PRECARN Incorporated

B: VIEWS FROM THE INFORMATION AND COMMUNICATION TECHNOLOGY SECTOR

THE ENGAGEMENT PROCESS

Research institutions, high-technology equipment manufacturers, software developers, telephone/cable providers, public agencies, professional associations and standards-based organizations all form part of the information and communication technology (ICT) community. The ICT sector comprises some of Canada's leading innovators, responsible for 20 percent of Canada's gross domestic product growth over the last five years. The core of the community is firms that manufacture equipment, develop software and applications, and provide services. Together, these firms employ 4 percent of Canadians, contribute

6 percent of gross domestic product, and perform 45 percent of industrial R&D.

E-business applications and processes are driving productivity growth in all industry sectors. In the United States, it is estimated that these applications will account for 40 percent of productivity growth over the next 10 years. Indeed, this sector reaches into every aspect of our economy and society, from culture to resources; from manufacturing to the retail and service sectors; from pre-school to post-secondary education; and from health care delivery to public sector services.

"If there is one thing the federal government can do to advance Canada's capacity for innovation, it should be to foster the widespread and rapid adoption of productivity-enhancing technology. We believe this goal is so fundamental it deserves a specifically stated set of targets of its own. One possible target would be: by 2010, raise the rate of investment in ICT throughout the economy to prevailing U.S. levels."

Information Technology Association of Canada

In recognition of the role played by members of the ICT sector, and the contributions they make to Canada's innovative capacity, Industry Canada conducted a separate consultations exercise with the ICT sector. A cross-section of the community, totalling some 50 companies, organizations and associations, was invited to participate. Participants spanned large and small commercial interests, leading research organizations, applications and content developers, and organizations active in education and community development. More than 40 stakeholders responded, either through formal submissions or bilateral discussions.

GENERAL IMPRESSIONS

By and large, ICT sector responses were consistent. They were unanimous in supporting the overall goals of the *Innovation Strategy*, agreeing that innovation should be a national priority, and supporting the policy directions put forward in the *Achieving Excellence* and *Knowledge Matters* documents. They shared many of the same views about Canada's innovation challenges, and had an equally high level of consensus about what needs to be done to create a culture of innovation. To create this culture of innovation, ICT stakeholders believe government, the private sector, the academic community, the education system and other parts of civil society must be equally committed and actively involved; that networking and communication across these communities is essential; and that the roles and responsibilities of different players in the innovation "system" must be clear. On the latter point, they stressed that government's role is to create an environment in which marketplace and social innovation can flourish. For example, stakeholders felt that governments should:

- Support the development of Canada's knowledge and skill base;

- Create competitive tax and regulatory regimes that favour innovation;

- Be a demanding customer for Canadian ICT products and services in order to improve their own productivity while supporting industrial innovation;

- Exercise policy leadership; and

- Celebrate successes and communicate the importance of innovation to all Canadians.

Meanwhile, there was consensus that marketplace innovation is the private sector's role. Participants believed this innovation should include building and expanding Canada's broadband networks and services, the infrastructure of the global information economy; commercializing research undertaken in university and government laboratories; developing productivity-enhancing technologies, applications and services; and promoting the diffusion and use of information and communication technology in all business sectors.

Finally, ICT stakeholders believed that the not-for-profit sector has a key role in applying and using ICT to support social innovation (for example, in education and health care), and to develop the innovative potential of physical and virtual communities. Furthermore, they believe there are opportunities for partnerships between government, the private sector and the not-for-profit sector in strategic areas such as developing policies and strategies; moving ideas through the innovation process from R&D to applications; enriching education; and ensuring that all Canadians have opportunities to participate in, and benefit from, an innovation culture. For example, sectors could work together to extend high-speed broadband connectivity to rural, remote and Aboriginal communities.

RESEARCH, DEVELOPMENT AND COMMERCIALIZATION

Participants supported proposals in the *Innovation Strategy* to strengthen private sector, university and government R&D, and to improve the commercialization of research undertaken in all these sectors. Furthermore, they saw a key opportunity for partnership and collaboration between these sectors via "fourth pillar" organizations supporting R&D partnerships to improve Canada's track record in the commercial application of knowledge. However, they had concerns about whether the R&D targets in *Achieving Excellence* are realistic and sufficiently focussed. While generally supporting the goal of moving Canada up in the world's R&D rankings, some believed that moving Canada from 15th place to among the top five by 2010 is not achievable given the huge increase in financial and human resources required. Others pointed to the omission of non-R&D-based innovation, such as innovations that arise when ICTs are applied by businesses and others to improve the productivity of production processes, supply chain management, and customer or client service delivery. While traditional R&D indicators and targets may not take these types of service innovations into account, they have a direct impact on Canada's productivity and its ability to remain globally competitive. Despite these concerns, stakeholders were eager to move forward as quickly as possible, and made a number of specific recommendations on what needs to be done.

> *"Introduce the emerging field of management of technological innovation and change to a broader cross-section of Canadians by developing broadly based undergraduate courses in technology management; creating exploratory applications research to anticipate market reactions; fostering effective science and technology communications; moving towards a transformative civil infrastructure centre; and advancing plans for a national biometric technology infrastructure."*
>
> University of Waterloo

Research and development

ICT corporate stakeholders, led by companies such as Nortel Networks, IBM Canada and March Networks, reaffirmed their commitment to remaining Canada's leading sector for industrial R&D. They are optimistic about the future, in spite of the current worldwide downturn in demand for telecommunications network equipment. They assume that, as a result of the *Innovation Strategy*, governments at all levels will ensure that Canada remains an attractive place to invest and create businesses. They emphasized that creating the right environment means more than ensuring that Canada's R&D incentives and tax regimes are competitive; it also means maintaining our quality of life. At the end of the day, it is people who innovate, and Canada must remain a place where people want to live.

Stakeholders also pointed to new challenges and opportunities that are emerging as a result of structural changes in the way R&D is done in the ICT sector, and to the need to ensure critical expertise and knowledge is not lost as a result of the current industry downturn. This restructuring is characterized by a shift from large, industrial R&D plants to innovation clusters that bring together small and medium-sized enterprises, large firms, universities and governments. Unless this opportunity is seized, stakeholders stated that Canada cannot sustain performance at the current level in private sector R&D, much less achieve the incremental increases called for in the *Innovation Strategy* targets. Stakeholders point to new innovation opportunities that are emerging as thousands of highly qualified R&D personnel, released from large firms that have traditionally done the lion's share of ICT R&D, take their expertise into small companies or start their own. In the context of innovation clusters, these highly qualified people and their small and medium-sized businesses are playing an increasingly pivotal role in innovation performance, as large firms are depending on them for more of their R&D (that is, through outsourcing), and university and government labs rely on them to facilitate commercialization.

Participating ICT stakeholders emphasized that facilitating the transformation of R&D in their sector requires new approaches to issues such as technology transfer and intellectual property rights, particularly as innovation clusters replace large firms, and as angel investors and venture capitalists, upon whom small and medium-sized businesses typically rely, become an increasingly important source of overall R&D investment funding. The transformation also highlights the importance of emerging issues such as the development of R&D capacity within small and medium-sized businesses (for example, open standards and open source software).

Suggested measures to deal with knowledge creation issues included creating partnerships to facilitate the redeployment of highly qualified personnel to start-ups, small and medium-sized enterprises, other industry sectors and academia. Participating stakeholders also called for a comprehensive approach by government to the policy, regulatory and standards issues that affect technology transfer and commercialization (such as open standards, open source software, spectrum allocation, copyright, etc.), thereby making R&D a worthwhile undertaking.

Commercialization

According to participants, an immediate priority in commercialization is strengthening the role of "fourth pillar" R&D organizations in strategic technology areas. These are organizations that create and manage R&D partnerships in order to move technology as seamlessly as possible from R&D to the application stage and on to commercialization in Canadian and foreign markets. Participants suggested this could be accomplished by:

- Building on the experience already developed in the Canadian Microelectronics Corporation, intelligent systems (for example, through PRECARN) and advanced networking (for example, through CANARIE), bringing Canada's strengths to the "next level" in these areas, and pursue this same approach to new, emerging core technology areas, such as high-performance computing and advanced optical and wireless broadband; and

- Following through on the proposals and commitments of leading research universities to improve the transfer and commercialization of knowledge from their labs by implementing technology incubators and accelerators (which would also help foster innovation clusters), through education and training, and by establishing a national network of university technology transfer offices.

With respect to the specific federal government programs that support the commercialization of Canadian R&D, participating ICT stakeholders recommended clearer mandates, and even consolidation, in order to improve their overall efficiency and reduce barriers to participation. They also suggested that the federal government support Export Development Canada in increasing its international marketing of Canadian ICTs, that it increase the number of trade commissioners assigned to this task, and that federal government operations themselves do more to showcase innovative Canadian products and services through a more proactive procurement policy.

Finally, participants believe that, in addition to its current focus on the commercialization of R&D, *Canada's Innovation Strategy* should be expanded to include a much stronger emphasis on the diffusion, application and management of productivity-enhancing technologies in all economic and social sectors. They pointed out that, while classical R&D-based innovation is well understood, little is known about innovation based on ICT-enabled improvements that enhance production processes, supply chain management, and the way businesses operate and public services are delivered. However, what is known suggests that the widening productivity gap between Canada and the United States is due, at least in part, to the greater adoption of ICTs by U.S. firms, including the recent adoption of Internet-based e-business processes. ICT stakeholders suggested that the innovation framework be expanded to include goals, targets, policy priorities and metrics specifically concerning the challenges of diffusing, applying and managing productivity-enhancing ICTs in all business sectors, and in the delivery of public services.

INNOVATION ENVIRONMENT

ICT stakeholders suggested that government can play an important role in fostering an innovation environment by working with stakeholders through groups such as the Canadian e-Business Initiative. Some participants called for more emphasis on the impact of trade and competition on stimulating innovation. They urged consideration of Canada's unique economic profile, such as the prevalence of resource-based industries, and the high proportion of small and medium-sized enterprises in our economic mix. They emphasized that this means we need to think "outside the box," seeing innovation as a process of using ICT to improve the productivity of business processes, public services and market access for small and medium-sized enterprises, at least as much as the invention of new products and processes.

Tax measures

ICT stakeholders support measures to ensure that Canada's corporate and personal tax policies are internationally competitive. They made a large number of specific suggestions for improving Canada's tax regime, including:

- Improving scientific research and experimental development tax credits (for example, by making them refundable); and broadening accessibility to companies, whether national or global, private or public, in manufacturing, software or service development.

- Ending federal taxation of provincial R&D credits.

- Eliminating taxes on capital investments.

- Accelerating depreciation on ICT equipment.

- Creating tax incentives for corporations to apply productivity-enhancing technologies.

- Introducing ICT training tax credits for individuals and/or corporations.

Regulatory reform

Participants strongly supported the *Innovation Strategy* commitment to review all Government of Canada regulatory regimes, and urged that the ICT sector be a priority. They believed that government should immediately review:

- Telecommunications policy and regulations, particularly the Government of Canada's foreign ownership rules and spectrum management policies, practices and fees.

- Selected Canadian Radio-television Communications Commission decisions and procedures, in order to eliminate barriers to investment, innovation and competition; and

- Copyright laws, where they believe that the balance struck between creators' rights and users' obligations in areas such as the use of ICT to record cultural content should be examined to ensure it does not unduly impede innovation.

From a longer-term perspective, ICT stakeholders would like government to undertake a fundamental review of the regulatory framework for their sector to address issues such as the balance between regulation and reliance on market forces; the elimination of asymmetrical regulation of industries offering competing services; and the potential restructuring of the federal regulatory apparatus to move responsibility for telecommunications, broadcasting and copyright into one, streamlined body.

SKILLED WORK FORCE

ICT stakeholders were concerned that skills targets may not be sufficiently detailed or strategically connected to other parts of the *Innovation Strategy*. For instance, to increase admission rates for students in post-graduate studies, they pointed out, it is necessary to have a larger pool of undergraduates to draw on. This, in turn, will require universities to attract larger numbers of faculty, for which they will require additional funding for university research.

In their submissions, ICT stakeholders made a number of creative proposals to develop, retain and attract the highly qualified personnel required to conduct world-class research, support commercialization, and optimize the redeployment of talent as a result of changes under way in ICT R&D. In addition, they made proposals to foster and attract skills in order to apply productivity-enhancing technologies in every economic and social sector. These proposals include:

- Student entrepreneurship programs;

- Enhanced co-op programs, including at the graduate level, that attract the best and brightest students from around the world;

- University-level courses in technology management, knowledge and innovation;

- ICT apprenticeship and professional certification programs in the private sector;

- Programs to assess and certify the ICT skills of immigrants;

- ICT training tax credits; and

- Expansion of eCorps, which helps small and medium-sized enterprises improve productivity through applying ICT-based e-business models and processes.

Aligning the learning system to reflect labour market needs

In general, participating ICT stakeholders supported the broad skills and learning agenda set out in the *Knowledge Matters* paper to improve educational outcomes in K-12, increase access to high-quality post-secondary education, and improve the skill levels and adaptability of Canada's work force. They recommended providing distance education opportunities at every level, from primary to post-graduate; providing on-line learning opportunities to support lifelong skills development; and promoting e-content literacy.

STRENGTHENING COMMUNITIES

The ICT sector feels strongly that the crucial ingredient for all communities to strengthen their innovation performance is access to high-speed broadband networks. This would not only support new business opportunities, but also create new ways of accessing education, health care and other public services. Here, they saw the main role of government as a customer for broadband networks and services, in order to deliver public services to rural, remote and Aboriginal communities. They see the private sector's role as one of building this infrastructure and offering services to government, businesses and residential customers.

While unanimously supporting the Government of Canada's broadband access target, participants had concerns about the target of developing at least 10 internationally recognized clusters by 2010. They pointed out that clusters generally emerge organically, from a serendipitous mix of many elements, including research, business acumen, social and cultural conditions, and lifestyle opportunities. Instead of attempting to create clusters, they believe government should focus on supporting them once they emerge. Furthermore, a number of stakeholders suggested having 10 world-class clusters may be too ambitious a goal for a country of Canada's size, and that a target for "successful in Canada" clusters may be more realistic.

CHAPTER 7

WHAT WE HEARD FROM SMALL AND MEDIUM-SIZED BUSINESSES

THE ENGAGEMENT PROCESS

Small and medium-sized businesses are the engine for Canada's economic growth. There are about 2.3 million small and medium-sized enterprises (SMEs) in Canada. According to Statistics Canada data, more than 75 percent of these firms employ five or fewer employees, whereas only 0.03 percent of all Canadian firms employ 500 people or more. SMEs account for more than half of the private sector labour force and the small business share of job creation has been steadily increasing over the past five years. In fact, small businesses (those with fewer than 100 employees) were responsible for 65 percent of the net new jobs created over the past two years.[1] Clearly, this group of companies plays a significant role in job creation and productivity growth in Canada.

Early in 2002, Industry Canada began exploring ways that it could increase the participation of SMEs in the engagement process for *Canada's Innovation Strategy*. The goal was to find a way that these businesses could easily feed into the process without having to travel or take too much time away from the demands of their day-to-day operations.

In June, an e-mail was sent to the chief executive officers of thousands of companies registered with Canadian Company Capabilities.[2] Companies were invited to complete an abbreviated on-line survey. The survey was also highlighted on the Strategis Web site, Industry Canada's link to the business community. Survey participants were asked to describe their perspectives on the top three innovation challenges faced by SMEs and to suggest their top three actions for addressing these challenges, according to each of four major themes — creating new knowledge and bringing it to market more quickly; developing skills for the new economy; setting the right business and regulatory environment; and strengthening communities across Canada.

---

1. *Industry Canada. Small Business Quarterly. Vol. 4, No. 2 (October 2002).*

2. *Canadian Company Capabilities, available through Strategis, is the main Industry Canada data base supporting several hundred on-line company directories. About 50 000 companies have been registered in the Canadian Companies Capabilities system. These data are compiled from companies who voluntarily provide it in order to participate in various Government of Canada initiatives to promote and market Canadian goods and services. Companies invited by e-mail to participate in the Innovation Strategy consultations had updated their information since April 1, 2001; were identified by Industry Canada operating units as belonging to one or more recognized industry sectors; and had provided corporate e-mail addresses to receive information from the Government of Canada.*

A total of 470 survey responses were received. While not statistically representative of Canadian industry, these responses provide an excellent source of detailed input from 470 Canadians, 82 percent of whom represent a large and varied cross-section of the SME target group that Industry Canada was hoping to reach.

In terms of regional representation, nearly half of the responses were from Ontario; 15 percent from Quebec; 14 percent from British Columbia; 13 percent from Alberta, Saskatchewan and Manitoba; 8 percent from the Atlantic provinces; and less than 1 percent from the territories. More than 87 percent of responses were from firms with 50 or fewer employees. More than 27 percent of respondents were from the services sector, 18 percent from the high-technology field, and slightly more than 15 percent from the manufacturing sector. Representation from other sectors, such as natural resources, transportation, construction and finance, made up between 1 and 3 percent each.

Industry Canada staff segregated and analyzed survey data according to major themes, and reviewed each comment. Analysts also performed secondary data analysis to assess how often specific issues were raised.

In addition to contributing via the survey, a number of SMEs made their own submissions, all of which reinforced the major points made by companies in the survey. A description of the challenges and actions for each section of the survey is presented below in order of frequency. This survey was in addition to the many SMEs who participated in regional summits and roundtables.

RESEARCH, DEVELOPMENT AND COMMERCIALIZATION

A crosscutting theme in many of the SME submissions was participants' sense of isolation, both from the policy-making process and from government economic development programs. Many SMEs felt that larger companies receive disproportionate amounts of the government's time, attention and funding assistance. There was also a concern that companies outside Ontario and Quebec do not receive equitable attention.

Overall, there was consensus about the need for governments to simplify access to programs and information, and to focus on a smaller number of strategic priorities. Government programs and services were viewed as too complex and administratively burdensome to access, making them of little real help to SMEs.

In terms of priorities, urban firms tended to be more focussed on the commercialization of R&D, whereas rural firms were more concerned about equity and access issues, including the need to exploit technology and improve access to information and learning opportunities.

> "*Industry will take the lead role in establishing a pilot 'resource centre,' which would provide information, assessment, unbiased advice, learning and project management for SME manufacturers.*"
>
> Canadian Manufacturing Process Sector

Challenges

Individual firms' submissions highlighted the "incredible hurdle" that commercialization represents. Getting innovative products from idea to market can be very difficult. This concern reinforced the need for far more collaboration between academic institutions, private investors, corporations and government to bring new products from concept to customer. SMEs raised nearly a dozen basic issues in the survey relating to the challenge of creating knowledge and bringing it to market. The top five were:

- *The need for sustainable levels of funding and support for SMEs, including non-financial support such as marketing assistance and export information.* Individual submissions highlighted the need for financial assistance to offset the direct costs involved in technology implementation (for example, in using e-business applications), and innovative tax incentives to ensure access to venture capital.

- *The need for government leadership and reforms to improve efficiency, reduce the regulatory burden, and bring about greater harmonization between levels of government.* Firms were concerned that government may be active in more areas than necessary, often competing with the private sector. Individual submissions highlighted the need for government to play a stronger role as "model user," encouraging the development and application of innovative Canadian technologies.

- *Uneven information flow between governments and businesses/Canadians related to economic data, trade/market opportunities, and business opportunities in general.* Firms pointed to the need to more fully exploit the Internet to improve access to strategic information, from which small firms felt particularly excluded.

- *The need for culture change to support innovation.* Firms noted a general mindset of complacency among industry, government and the general population regarding the need for an innovation agenda and action plan. They commented that Canadians tend to be content to pursue incremental changes rather than bold, new innovations, particularly from SMEs, which appears to be a strength of direct competitors in the United States.

- *The need for improvements in education and training, in both the academic and vocational streams.* Many SMEs felt that the education system desperately needs to be revamped, especially in terms of creating more forward-focussed curricula, providing sustained funding, and providing more lifelong learning opportunities in the workplace.

Suggested actions

While respondents suggest 16 areas of action, the five most frequently mentioned were:

- *Selective incentives*. SMEs felt that financial and non-financial assistance is required to address the knowledge challenge. This assistance would include tax credits, loans and grants, as well as marketing assistance, management support, export information, and access to government information. Respondents also pointed out that financial assistance should be focussed on a more limited number of opportunities, and application processes should be simplified to accommodate smaller companies. Individual submissions praised the Industrial Research Assistance Program, but highlighted the need to increase its efficiency and the number of counselors it provides to small businesses, and expand its reach.

- *Government action in vision, leadership and efficiency*. Many respondents mentioned an apparent lack of coordination between levels of government, and between departments and agencies within governments. They felt a clearer vision and direction are essential, along with a collaborative and coordinated approach that involves private sector and academic partners. They also felt strongly that existing systems, processes and regulations should be reviewed, and, where they are unduly onerous or duplicative, reduced or eliminated.

- *More focus and support, and better standards for education/training*. Many respondents felt that there needs to be more cooperation between provinces, and greater involvement by the federal government, in setting agendas and standards to improve the education system nationwide. Others felt there must be more apprenticeship and technology-oriented education opportunities, as well as strategic generalist programs.

- *Enhancing communication and information flows between all levels*. SMEs noted that access to government information in particular should be free of charge. They also encouraged better information flow and exchange of ideas between government, academia and the business community.

- *More partnerships and networks among all stakeholders*. SMEs shared the view that, for them, developing and commercializing products and services, particularly on a global scale, requires partnerships to spread the risk, exchange expertise and create synergies in areas such as marketing and distribution. Many survey participants noted that smaller R&D companies had particular difficulties in successfully commercializing new ideas without a broader support network. A number of respondents felt that focussed development of virtual clusters was the best path to creating these partnerships and overcoming barriers such as geography, and that such networks should include government, academia and the private sector.

SKILLED WORK FORCE

Again, the themes of isolation, complexity, and lack of coordination between and within governments dominated SMEs' critiques of Canada's education and training system, and were major themes in the submissions from individual businesses.

Challenges

In total, respondents identified 17 basic challenges in this area. The four most frequently mentioned were:

- *The need to refocus and support education and training.* SMEs were very critical of the current state of Canada's education and training system. Specific concerns included outdated course materials, a weak focus on emerging opportunities, aging professors, the prohibitive cost of tuition, and underuse of e-learning opportunities. While recognizing the need for lifelong learning, SMEs were concerned that, without government assistance or incentives, the costs of providing vocational training to employees would be prohibitive. While they agreed that a more focussed immigration policy could help alleviate immediate skills shortfalls, they emphasized that Canada's education and training system needs to be revamped. Individual business submissions emphasized the need to look to underused talent pools, such as women, Aboriginal people, immigrants, persons with disabilities, displaced workers, and at-risk youth.

- *The need for new thinking/culture change.* SMEs felt that there is a general state of complacency about the need for a skills development agenda. Respondents said that too much attention is focussed on local markets and issues, and not enough on emerging opportunities in the global economy. There was also concern about the lack of nationwide standards in education. Individual business submissions emphasized the need for Canada to produce more science graduates.

- *Difficulties in attracting and retaining skilled workers.* SME representatives felt the main reasons for this were a lack of challenging employment opportunities in innovative areas, and, particularly, lower wages and higher personal taxes compared to the U.S. However, SMEs also said that a general lack of understanding about Canada's advantages is making it difficult both to retain qualified workers and attract skilled immigrants.

- *Uneven and conflicting qualifications and standards, particularly differences in standards and qualifications between provinces.* Many SME representatives said this makes it difficult to recruit consistently qualified labour and capitalize on immigrants' skills. SMEs also pointed to a perceived "closed mind" attitude on the part of some labour and professional bodies that restricts qualified immigrants from working at a level commensurate with their education and training.

Suggested actions

In total, respondents identified 16 general actions that they felt would better position Canada's labour force for the future. The four most frequently mentioned were:

- *Refocussing university, college and vocational training on existing and future labour force requirements.* Individual business submissions suggested establishing new, industry-led training corporations to champion and oversee training for trades and technical skills; creating a better system to promote trade and technical schools; and creating a new funding mechanism to enable industry and academic institutions to obtain assistance to establish more co-op programs.

- *Providing focussed incentives for companies and individuals.* Employers and individuals should be offered assistance, including tax credits, loans and grants, to help overcome the barriers posed by rising tuition costs and lack of time, as well as non-financial support, such as access to training material, e-learning resources, networked information, etc.

- *Collecting and disseminating information on future skills requirements.* SMEs recommend that this information be publicized and used to redesign education and vocational training programs, and to optimize the use of e-learning. Broader use of e-learning was a particularly popular theme among rural SMEs, who felt excluded from the education and vocational skills development systems. In addition, there were a number of recommendations against developing university and college programs at the expense of giving more attention to technical and apprenticeship skills development, which many felt was needed.

- *Coordinating government action in terms of vision, leadership and efficiency.* Again, SMEs pointed to a perceived lack of coordinated, future-focussed leadership by governments. Many suggested that governments should consider encouraging greater participation by private sector and academic partners on education, skills development, and regulation and strategy development. Respondents tended to see government's role in this area as centred on forecasting future skills demands and instituting a more focussed immigration policy to help address skills shortages.

STRENGTHENING COMMUNITIES

Many of the same issues mentioned elsewhere, such as isolation and lack of influence over policy and decision making, were mentioned by SME representatives.

Challenges

SME representatives mentioned a total of 30 issue areas in relation to enabling communities to develop and exploit knowledge and expertise, attract investment, and create a critical mass of innovative capabilities. The five most frequently mentioned were:

- *Lack of collaboration, dialogue, harmonization and cooperation between levels of government and with the public.* This exacerbates the mounting difficulties SMEs face in obtaining financing and attracting the skills they need to pursue and exploit emerging opportunities. They identified dealing with multiple levels of government — each with their own regulations and policies, and differing agendas and priorities — as a significant challenge. They also felt there is uneven access to current government information. Many SMEs outside Ontario and Quebec felt they were isolated from government policy makers.

- *Lack of community vision and leadership.* SMEs cited a narrow, local focus among local politicians as an impediment to positioning their community to partner with other communities and levels of government to take advantage of emerging opportunities.

- *Inadequate access to broadband, especially in northern and remote areas.* This was cited as a major challenge to the ability of communities to pursue business networking/information exchange, education/skills development and improved access to health care, as well as to participate fully in the political, economic and innovation agendas of the country. SMEs felt that without government support to bring broadband to communities it would not happen, or would happen too slowly.

- *Inequitable attention by governments to different regions, particularly remote communities and centres outside Ontario and Quebec.* Many respondents felt that more remote communities were less likely to be aware or take advantage of government programs. Many respondents felt that the lack of non-financial government assistance (collaborative networks, access to information) was even more of a problem than accessing a proportionate share of government financial assistance.

- *Inadequate social development programs to address localized challenges.* High unemployment, health care and education shortfalls, uneven and inequitable access to information resources, an overreliance on resource extraction, an underuse of otherwise qualified immigrants, and skills deficiencies were all cited as challenges to be addressed. SME representatives felt that, while national programs may provide some value to a wide constituency, they offer little to address issues unique to the individual communities.

Suggested actions

Respondents made more than 30 recommendations for actions, of which the three most frequently mentioned were:

- *Bringing broadband access to the community level for business, social and educational purposes.* SME representatives felt this should involve government assistance and would render many additional "public good" benefits. This recommendation was also strongly endorsed in submissions from individual businesses. Affordable broadband access would enable all communities to participate more fully in the economic, social and innovation agendas of the nation.

- *Increasing dialogue, harmonization and cooperation between levels of government and with the public.* Collaborative partnership networks involving large and small firms, government and academia, were seen as essential in order to spread risk and find synergies related to expertise, distribution and marketing networks. A number of participants suggested that focussed development of virtual clusters was probably the best way to capitalize on strengths regardless of geography, overcome the difficulties of economies of scale and provide more equitable opportunities for regional participation.

- *Building community vision and leadership.* Many survey respondents suggested that local politicians must increase their awareness of regional, provincial, national and even global opportunities, if community innovation capacity is to be strengthened. In addition, SMEs recommended that there be more autonomy at the community level, along with greater attention to aging and inadequate physical infrastructure, such as transportation links.

REGULATORY AND TAX ENVIRONMENT

The themes of isolation, undue complexity and inefficiency in government programs and regulatory regimes, and the need for greater coordination between governments and more partnerships involving the private sector and academia, again dominated SME comments.

Challenges

SMEs raised a total of 10 challenges to optimizing Canada's business and regulatory environment in order to improve our innovation performance. The four most frequently mentioned were:

- *Lack of government leadership.* SMEs felt that a lack of coordination between levels of government, and between different government departments and agencies and a number of regulations inhibited their innovation potential.

- *Excessive, confusing and contradictory regulations.* SMEs felt a complex regulatory structure put them at a particular disadvantage compared to larger firms and U.S. competitors. Many SMEs do not approach or make use of government assistance programs because of the regulatory overhead.

- *Taxes.* SMEs strongly felt that taxes were excessive in Canada compared to the United States, and put them at a disadvantage compared to larger firms in Canada, which they felt were better able to take advantage of tax breaks.

- *A weak focus on SMEs in terms of government attention and assistance.* Respondents said they felt less able than larger firms to influence governments' policy agendas and program design. They felt that a number of larger companies, especially in Ontario and Quebec, were receiving a disproportionate amount of governments' attention and support. They also said they were less likely to take advantage of government programs and services because of non-SME-friendly requirements (for example, programs and services that are too costly and complex). For example, many mentioned having to pay for Statistics Canada data.

> "*Canada needs to improve the rate of conversion of innovation to product and product-ready technology. The innovation agenda must pay more attention to the technology transfer process, if small and medium industries are to make effective use of research instruments.*"
>
> . Dr. Robert Crawhall,
> National Capital Institute of Telecommunications

Suggested actions

Respondents provided a total of 16 general actions to help create a business and regulatory environment in Canada that is more conducive to SME innovation. The five most frequent suggestions made were:

- *Reviewing and reducing taxes, particularly the corporate and personal tax burden, and reducing or eliminating the Capital Tax and the goods and services tax.* Tax holidays were suggested for the early commercialization phase of innovative new products. Respondents also suggested tax equity and uniformity across all Canadian jurisdictions, and an overall simplification of the tax system. In individual submissions, businesses suggested creating a human resource investment tax credit for businesses and individuals who invest in education and training. They also praised the scientific research and experimental development tax credit, but recommended that the carry forward be extended over a longer time horizon to more accurately reflect how long it takes to get a new product to market and turn a profit. Finally, they suggested specific tax-based incentives to get knowledge to market faster, and pointed to Quebec as an example and, specifically, to that province's refundable tax credit on R&D contracted to universities. They also suggested a five-year exemption from provincial tax for foreign scientists.

- *Creating freer trade.* SMEs recommended the elimination, if possible, or otherwise the harmonization of all existing interprovincial trade regulations/barriers, as well as those between Canada and the United States (that is, under the North American Free Trade Agreement [NAFTA]). SMEs also requested efforts to ensure that NAFTA trade dispute rulings are more equitable with respect to Canada, and that the government does more to provide them with market information and to facilitate the sharing of marketing expertise.

- *Reviewing and reducing regulations.* SME representatives felt this should apply in all areas, with regulations being reduced or eliminated if they do not provide clear benefits. Respondents felt that regulations should be simplified and regulation regimes consolidated between levels of government. They suggested that collaborative boards involving the private and public sectors could assist this redesign. Individual submissions stressed that Canada must have a more responsive regulatory system that is science-based and makes decisions faster, suggesting a 12-month maximum time frame.

- *Improving government leadership.* This included facilitating the participation of the private sector and academic partners in program, regulation and strategy design and delivery, and improving information dissemination to help ease concerns about equity and transparency. Individual submissions emphasized the need for more action by government as a first-time user of innovative new Canadian technologies and products. They pointed to the Department of National Defence's current policy favouring off-the-shelf procurement, which they said exploits innovations occurring abroad instead of encouraging made-in-Canada innovations.

- *Providing more SME-focussed programs and services that would be more conducive to SME needs and abilities to comply.*

CHAPTER 8

WHAT WE HEARD FROM THE ACADEMIC COMMUNITY

THE ENGAGEMENT PROCESS

The academic community is the primary driver of knowledge creation and advanced learning in Canada. It includes universities and colleges, research institutes, libraries, and a host of other institutions, networks, and advocacy groups that have a stake in Canada's higher education system. Also included are tens of thousands of teaching and research professionals, managers and administrators, and several million full- and part-time learners. Within each segment of the academic community, organizations and umbrella groups have formed to share ideas and concerns, and to advance the interests of their members. For example, the Association of Canadian Community Colleges has 153 member institutions, the Canadian Library Association represents 3000 institutions and individual members, and the Graduate Students' Association of Canada speaks on behalf of more than 80 000 students enrolled in master's and PhD programs.

To give the academic community a voice in *Canada's Innovation Strategy*, Industry Canada and HRDC invited feedback from associations and individual institutions on the policy directions and challenges outlined in the two papers. During the spring and summer of 2002, 25 formal submissions were received. To seek further input, HRDC sponsored a number of best practices workshops on education and learning issues in centres across Canada.

GENERAL IMPRESSIONS

Submissions from the academic community generally supported the analysis and milestones set out in the *Knowledge Matters* and *Achieving Excellence* documents. For example, proposals aimed at increasing graduate student enrolment, extending broadband access in all regions, and improving Aboriginal participation in higher learning were broadly endorsed. At the same time, academic community leaders had a number of concerns. Some thought, for instance, that the definitions of innovation and commercialization were too narrow. Several believed government must do more to recognize the critical importance of early childhood development as the starting point for all learning and future work force development. Others called for longer time frames for achieving goals for adult and post-secondary education. There was also a further, overarching concern — that Canadians need to learn more about innovation and why it is important before they will embrace it as a national priority.

Submissions from specific groups making up the academic community emphasized different priorities. For example, universities placed first priority on increased levels of research funding, funding for indirect costs of research, increased capacity to meet the demand for highly qualified people, and support for commercialization efforts. Research institutes are primarily concerned about the existing capacity to commercialize research, particularly the lack of skills and people to meet the challenge (for example, business-savvy technologists and technicians, knowledge brokers and incubator managers), and the need for greater collaboration among researchers. Colleges wanted a national program for technical and vocational education, greater links between the labour force and education system (for example, apprenticeship programs, on-line learning programs) and the right to be eligible for research funding from the granting councils. Professional institutes were primarily concerned about skill sets, especially the lack of management and leadership skills among small and medium-sized enterprise owners and their limited knowledge of available technology for manufacturing and marketing. Learners were greatly concerned about the cost of education and thus focussed on possible solutions through changes to the Canada Student Loans Program and "learner" tax credits.

> *"Universities are ready and willing to build on their already impressive contribution. They are eager to perform more research, to produce even more highly qualified graduates, and to play an even more central role in empowering their communities through knowledge and innovation. Universities are committed to ensuring that more Canadians from traditionally disadvantaged groups, such as Aboriginal people, are able to obtain the benefits of higher education so that they — and their communities — can be players in the knowledge economy."*
>
> Association of Universities and Colleges of Canada

Academic leaders also pointed to issues that they believed had been overlooked in the *Achieving Excellence* and *Knowledge Matters* documents. At the top of their list was a lack of attention to student financing issues. A number of respondents also wanted the goal of increasing graduate enrolment tied more closely to academic infrastructure funding and other "capacity" issues. Some thought that the papers should have recognized the export potential of Canada's academic community and how participation in international education activities can stimulate innovation in Canada. Finally, representatives of Canada's libraries felt that the role of libraries in supporting formal, informal and lifelong learning, and in extending broadband to all communities, was not sufficiently recognized. They expressed their commitment to putting knowledge within reach of all Canadians and play a pivotal role in community-based initiatives.

RESEARCH, DEVELOPMENT AND COMMERCIALIZATION

Research and development

Academic leaders were unanimous in calling on both federal and provincial governments to substantially increase funding for colleges and universities. Specifically, they looked to the Government of Canada to double budgets for federal granting councils within 10 years, to extend support to college-based research, to create a permanent program to finance indirect costs of federally sponsored research, and to bring smaller universities more fully into the Canada Research Chairs Program. They felt that private industry should compensate universities for indirect research costs, and some suggested that a portion of these revenues should flow to research libraries.

Participants called on the provinces to boost core funding to support faculty recruitment and expand research and teaching capacity in colleges and universities. To improve efficiency and generate economies of scale, respondents urged government agencies and granting councils to standardize their selection processes and support packages, to simplify and accelerate application procedures, and to encourage university researchers to collaborate more and to integrate research strategies and programs.

"We will continue to commit resources for the development and support of our university technology transfer office."

Queen's University

There were concerns among university leaders that the *Innovation Strategy*'s focus on commercializing R&D might come at the expense of their mandates of basic and pure research. They also believed that the *Innovation Strategy* places too much emphasis on science and technology while overlooking the contribution of the social sciences and humanities. Teaching, research and learning within these disciplines not only account for 50 percent of faculty and 60 percent of students in Canadian universities, but are key to understanding the social, cultural and economic dimensions of innovation. What's more, the social sciences and humanities are the streams that will produce tomorrow's leaders in business, government and the arts.

University submissions also stressed that, to meet targets for growth in R&D, the Government of Canada and the provinces must address serious deferred maintenance and infrastructure issues. They called for a 10-year program for academic infrastructure renewal.

Commercialization

While welcoming the significant increase in government funding of R&D over the past two decades, academic leaders pointed out that there has been no parallel investment in commercialization capacity. As a result, universities, hospitals and other research institutions have not developed sufficient technology transfer expertise to take new knowledge out of their laboratories and into the marketplace. To address this weakness, university leaders called on government to establish a national "internship program" to equip research professionals with the full range of innovation management skills. They believed that, if implemented immediately, such a program could triple the number of commercialization specialists in Canada by 2006.

Leaders from research institutes were also concerned about Canada's capacity to commercialize research, and believed that the solution to the problem would involve new, broader graduate study programs. They recommended that part of any investment in graduate education be designated for programs that give students "strategic training experiences" and specifically nurture the skills and attributes needed to translate laboratory findings into marketable products and processes.

Academic leaders called for the creation of two new national and regional institutions to build commercialization capacity in Canada:

- A national alliance of regional innovation and technology commercialization centres that would be anchored in a network of community colleges, and provide support to small firms in areas such as product and process development, market intelligence and financing.

- A national network of knowledge transfer, incubation and entrepreneurship that would help universities, colleges and other research institutions to pool expertise and share best practices in marketing new knowledge, promoting entrepreneurialism and getting new start-up companies off the ground.

One of the major concerns of Canada's community colleges and technical institutes was their continued exclusion from funding by federal granting councils. Representatives from these institutions felt that this significantly limits their potential in both knowledge creation and commercialization.

Ensuring accessible post-secondary education

The strength of Canada's work force stems from the fact that it has one of the world's highest participation rates in post-secondary education. Protecting and enhancing accessibility to college and university study is a top priority for academic leaders, and key to the long-term success of the *Innovation Strategy*. With this in mind, they called for improvements to the Canada Student Loans Program, better harmonization with provincial programs, and for the federal government to implement the student debt reduction measures announced in its 1998 budget. Other suggestions for addressing student debt burdens included increasing tax deductions for loan payments, freezing debt and interest charges during periods of unemployment or underemployment, and lowering interest rates.

Groups representing learners, such as the Graduate Students' Association of Canada, were concerned that the bulk of new funding under the Canada Health and Social Transfer had been invested in health care, with very little going to education. They were disappointed by the lack of attention to accessibility issues such as student debt, the tax treatment of scholarship income and the need for changes to the Canada Student Loans Program. They also pointed out that the failure to extend financial aid to part-time learners was inconsistent with the objective of boosting adult learning. Colleges suggested that the Lifelong Learning Plan should allow part-time learners to access funds from their registered retirement savings plans to participate in learning programs.

At the Roundtable on Strengthening Accessibility and Excellence in Post-Secondary Education, universities, colleges, labour groups, businesses, First Nations representatives and governments expressed concerns that the combination of rising student costs and increasing competition for places would limit access for many groups, including Aboriginal Canadians, students from low-income families, and adult learners. There was broad consensus that participation in post-secondary education should be encouraged, but that the current system lacks the capacity to meet existing demand, let alone the 20- to 30-percent growth in demand foreseen over the next few years. Participants pointed out that these same groups of students tend to be excluded by the very high academic qualifications now required for entry into many over-subscribed programs. They discussed the need to develop a framework that would meet the learning needs of Canadians, and felt that this would not only require building additional capacity, but investing in the renewal and development of the current system. Participants also called for increased coordination of policies among institutions and across jurisdictions in order to improve the articulation of programs and the portability of credentials.

Input from the academic community also stressed the need for a more unified vision of learning in Canada. Some leaders, for example, called on the federal and provincial governments to sign a national accord on higher education and research. This would respect current jurisdictions, but commit both levels of governments to long-term goals and funding arrangements, allowing colleges, universities and research institutions to plan more effectively.

"Everyone was concerned about the cost of pursuing a post-secondary education. The debt load we are required to assume is daunting and overwhelming. We don't know what to do, what direction to take after high school, and don't want to spend a great deal of money on an education that might not serve us in the long term."

HRDC roundtable with youth

Ensuring accessible adult education

To ensure that working adults have access to learning opportunities, academic leaders called for improvements in financial assistance to adult part-time learners, tax incentives to encourage employers to deliver workplace training, and special measures to ensure that Aboriginal Canadians and other groups with special needs have access to continuous learning (for example, bridging programs). They also believed that adult learning programs must be more flexible, in order to meet the needs of working people, and less intimidating to people with no formal education beyond high school. Academic leaders also insisted that all forms of learning should be exempt from the goods and services tax.

One suggestion was to create a national "open university" offering special degree and diploma completion programs and housing a national accreditation body. Participants felt that, if prior learning assessment services were offered and existing skills and knowledge were recognized, adult learners would not have to "start at square one," and would be encouraged to enrol in post-secondary learning programs.

One theme that was common to all discussions of adult learning was that affordability is an essential prerequisite for accessibility. There was a suggestion, for example, that a society that believes in lifelong learning should offer financial assistance to part-time learners, as well as generous education leave. Others suggested the development of protocols for credit transfers between Canadian learning institutions. For many, however, the concept of an accessible adult learning system went further — it also implied that programs would be available to suit individual learning styles and to cater to people with family responsibilities. Others suggested a more flexible approach to defining part-time learning. In addition, many felt that the availability of prior learning assessment and recognition facilities would encourage adults to participate in formal skills upgrading programs.

Participants at the Roundtable on Strengthening Accessibility and Excellence in Post-Secondary Education recommended that ways be found for students, especially adult learners, to complete their studies efficiently and affordably. Many agreed that more importance should be placed on colleges and employer-based training within the overall post-secondary education system. Post-secondary learning in all its forms, from trades training to doctoral research, was seen to be a key factor in both economic growth and individual development.

At the e-learning best practices workshop, participants noted that many Aboriginal communities lack the necessary technology infrastructure to make e-learning accessible. At the same time, they said, there is a need to make Aboriginal content more readily available on-line. Participants also recognized that Canadians who are unfamiliar with information technology will be excluded from e-learning opportunities. Some suggested that a computer competency element be added to the traditional definition of functional literacy. Workshop participants also expressed a need for greater access to information about recognition of workplace learning, including program models and existing research. They suggested that this would help promote awareness and recognition of adult learning needs.

Submissions from the academic community also suggested that the *Innovation Strategy* must better recognize the potential of on-line learning if objectives for adult learning are to be achieved. Some called for a national advertising campaign to tell Canadians about the learning opportunities available over the Internet and the standards for on-line learning.

At the best practices workshop on literacy, participants strongly agreed on the need for a pan-Canadian literacy strategy involving all levels of government, businesses, labour, education, and training providers, as well as literacy groups and non-governmental organizations. Above all, they saw a need to raise awareness and promote understanding of literacy issues, and to develop and share best practices in connection with family and community-based literacy activities.

> " *International education is a two-way street. The benefits of hosting international students, researchers and academics on Canada's campuses include internationalization of the campus and community, introduction of international perspectives in the classroom, and enrichment of the research achievements of our institutions. Longer term, there are benefits for Canada when alumni look for trading partners in their former host environment.* "
>
> Canadian Bureau for International Education

Aligning the learning system to reflect labour market needs

Several submissions cautioned against overproducing PhDs when other skill sets are also in short supply. They suggested, for example, that businesses, especially small and medium-sized enterprises, need people with management, leadership and marketing skills coupled with an understanding of manufacturing technology. To address this demand, they called for a "corporate mentorship program" that would connect personnel in small firms with seasoned executives in larger operations for advice and counselling, particularly during the difficult start-up phase.

Colleges and technical institutes are the main suppliers of classroom training for the skilled trades. They are concerned, however, that a lack of national standards with respect to apprenticeships, and technical and vocational training is impeding labour mobility across provincial borders, and leading to skills shortages in some parts of the country. They called for a coordinated, national approach that would confer a "skills passport" to improve interprovincial mobility.

At the "Partnerships that Work!" event, there was particular interest expressed on the part of sector councils in collaborating with the education sector to ensure compatibility between curricula and labour market needs.

A key point to emerge from consultations with groups representing persons with disabilities is the need to build supports at the high school level to provide for smoother school to work transitions. These included training teachers to be aware of the issues that persons with disabilities will face in the labour market and incorporating this into guidance and career counselling programs.

Investing in international education

A number of submissions called on federal and provincial authorities to invest more in international education to stimulate a growing exchange of people and ideas between Canadian and foreign universities and colleges. One specific idea was for immigration authorities to make it easier for foreign students to work in Canada.

"In educational institutions, innovation is fostered and sustained by the use of the Internet. However, the existing Copyright Act impedes technology-enhanced learning. Currently, provisions of the Act are infringed when students and educators engage in routine activities such as forwarding e-mails and copying information for study purposes. The Act must be revised to legalize and promote technology-enhanced learning, allowing students and educators to employ Internet-based resources without breaking copyright law."

Association of Canadian Community Colleges

The academic community also indicated that support for their internationalization processes is crucial in ensuring that all students can develop and strengthen their international skills. They said that international education must include the development of international curricula, as well as agreements for the recognition and transfer of foreign credits.

Leaders also called upon governments to support and endorse the Campus Canada initiative, suggesting that extending Prior Learning Assessment and Recognition services to potential immigrants will help Canadian colleges and universities attract international students and will support Canada's immigration objectives. Further, they recommended that the federal government make it easier to streamline the work permit process and extend the duration of post-graduate employment from one to two years.

Encouraging science education

Knowledge Matters sets a goal of making Canada one of the top three nations in the world in science, mathematics and reading achievement among young learners. Yet, Canada is one of the few countries in the industrialized world with no national program to support science centres. Several submissions called for a national program to promote science education and to highlight the connection between science and technology education and innovation.

INNOVATION ENVIRONMENT

Regulatory reform

Copyright laws topped the list of regulatory concerns in the academic community. Leaders called for a clear framework that provides reasonable protection of intellectual property while meeting the needs of learners and researchers to have ready access to information. Libraries, in particular, were concerned that "digital copyright laws" should not limit the enormous potential of Internet-based learning by removing research and other material from the public domain. Educators called for an amendment to digital copyright laws to allow students and educators to make effective and legal use of publicly available Internet materials.

Taxation

Since Canada's academic institutions operate in a world market for learning and knowledge, participants felt that a competitive tax regime is essential for our colleges and universities to attract and retain the best and brightest minds, both as faculty and as students. With scholarships for top students now running as high as $15 000 per year, many submissions called for a substantial increase in the $3000 limit on tax-deductible scholarship income. Similarly, they noted that lower rates of personal income tax would make it easier to hire and hold onto top-flight faculty and staff from Canada and abroad.

Another suggestion was to change tax regulations to allow people to borrow from their registered retirement savings plans to cover learning expenses in the same way that they can to finance the purchase of a home.

Branding Canada

Academic leaders called for an international campaign to market Canada as "more than a resource economy." The campaign would highlight Canada's research achievements and capacity, as well as our economic strengths, and promote Canada as a good place to conduct and invest in research.

STRENGTHENING COMMUNITIES

The Campus Canadian Alliance represents 18 post-secondary institutions and is composed of three key organizations: the Canadian Virtual University, the Canadian Virtual College Consortium, and the Canadian Learning Bank of British Columbia's Open Learning Agency. Campus Canadian Alliance members will reduce restrictions on residency and ensure program quality by using existing and new credit transfer protocols between Campus Canadian Alliance institutions and the 75 universities and colleges promoting courses in the Campus Connection protocol.

Most academic leaders believed that Canadian colleges and universities are poorly networked into industrial clusters compared with their counterparts in Europe and the United States. They felt that steps must be taken by governments to encourage academic institutions to improve their capacity to participate in cooperative research partnerships that can form the nucleus for cluster formation.

Leaders from the library sector felt that their support for formal and informal learning, particularly in rural communities, has largely been overlooked in the *Innovation Strategy*. They are strongly committed to improving and strengthening Canada's knowledge infrastructure by developing their collections, services and technologies. Libraries not only make learning accessible to Canadians, they extend broadband coverage to small communities, and are the storehouse for much of Canada's knowledge. To strengthen community-based learning, academic leaders urged the federal government to sustain support for the Community Access Program and Community Learning Network, and make Canada's libraries the first-choice location for public Internet access facilities.

CHAPTER 9

DISCUSSIONS WITH PROVINCIAL AND TERRITORIAL GOVERNMENTS

THE ENGAGEMENT PROCESS

Provinces and territories are essential partners in addressing Canada's innovation challenges. The provincial and territorial governments have jurisdiction over education, and significant responsibilities for economic and social development, all of which play important roles in determining Canada's performance in skills and learning. Provincial and territorial tax and regulatory systems, industrial development incentives, research funding programs, and infrastructure policies profoundly influence the innovation environment.

> **"Federal–provincial–territorial governments agree on the goal of making Canada one of the most innovative countries in the world... Ministers recognize that this overarching goal cannot be met by government actions alone and call upon all players in the innovation system to play their part."**
>
> *Principles for Action,*
> Federal–Provincial–Territorial Science and Technology Ministerial Meeting, Québec, September 20–21, 2001

Since the release of *Canada's Innovation Strategy* in February 2002, HRDC and Industry Canada have engaged provinces and territories in discussing the respective papers through a series of government-to-government discussions.

INDUSTRY CANADA DISCUSSIONS WITH PROVINCES AND TERRITORIES

The Government of Canada recognizes that provincial and territorial governments already commit significant resources to fostering innovation in their jurisdictions. Consequently, Industry Canada sought the views of provincial and territorial Deputy Ministers and Ministers responsible for industry, research, and science and technology on *Achieving Excellence* through two government-to-government multilateral meetings, and invited each province and territory to provide written comments on the *Innovation Strategy*. Federal–provincial–territorial deputy Ministers met in Ottawa on April 25–26, 2002, while Ministers met in Vancouver on June 20–21, 2002. The key ideas and concerns emerging from these discussions are summarized below.

Provincial and territorial governments supported the overall thrust of *Achieving Excellence*. A number of them pointed to existing policies and programs within their own jurisdictions that complement proposed national approaches. In fact, many provincial governments have launched processes or introduced their own innovation strategies. There was a clear recognition that building a culture of innovation in Canada will require a concerted and coordinated effort from all governments, and from other stakeholders in the public and private sectors. Provincial and territorial governments were fairly comfortable with the targets established in the *Innovation Strategy* and believed that they were useful in providing a sense of direction. However, some were thought to be somewhat ambitious. Smaller jurisdictions noted the particular challenges they will face in meeting the targets, since their innovation performance currently lags behind the larger provinces. These jurisdictions believed that the *Innovation Strategy* should expressly state the objective of closing the "innovation gap" between Canada's regions. Territorial governments noted their concerns that the targets did not speak to the particular economic challenges facing the North. In terms of implementation, Ministers called for a flexible, inclusive approach that would accommodate differences in provincial priorities and fiscal capacities, and allow goals and targets to be established on a regional basis.

Advice from Provinces and Territories

Ministers discussed the need for better coordination of federal and provincial investments in R&D to generate efficiencies and capitalize on existing strengths. Some jurisdictions felt that the structure of cost-shared programs could be improved to better take account of provinces' priorities and fiscal capacities. Ministers also clearly recognized that the private sector would need to greatly increase its expenditures on R&D in order to meet the targets. Thus, much of their discussion focussed on suggestions to:

- Improve the supply of angel investment for small, high-growth firms;

- Set more aggressive venture capital targets than those proposed in the *Innovation Strategy*, and establish regional goals as well (several jurisdictions indicated that they are looking at pension funds as potential sources of venture capital);

- Increase the potential of flow-through shares for fast-growth sectors such as biotechnology and life sciences.

A review of securities regulations to identify impediments to interprovincial flows of investment funds was suggested. Ministers also noted that colleges and technical institutes have great potential to promote innovation and, in particular, to help small firms adopt new production processes. They hoped this potential would be recognized and more fully exploited as the *Innovation Strategy* evolves.

The views of provincial and territorial Ministers were in line with those of industry and other groups in agreeing that the 2010 deadline for a comprehensive regulatory review proposed in the *Innovation Strategy* should be advanced. They also endorsed the idea of harmonizing regulations wherever possible across jurisdictions, and agreed to identify priority areas for reform, including securities regulations governing private placements.

Ministers also discussed the possibility of setting more aggressive targets for commercialization under the *Innovation Strategy* that would capture innovation through improved technology transfer and intellectual property processes. They also stressed the importance of strengthening the National Research Council Canada laboratories and the Industrial Research Assistance Program as initiatives to facilitate capacity building.

Provincial and territorial Ministers acknowledged the need for close cooperation among governments, and with the private sector to provide the infrastructure, skills and supportive business climate that will nurture real and virtual innovative clusters and centres of excellence. Several jurisdictions mentioned that they already have regional measures in place to promote the development of clusters, and that any new federal cluster incentives should build upon these strategies.

Provincial and territorial Ministers strongly agreed on the need to move quickly with innovative new programs to make high-speed broadband available to communities in all regions. They saw this as key to bridging the rural–urban digital divide and critically important to economic development in Canada's North.

Next steps

Ministers agreed to meet again following the National Summit on Innovation and Learning to discuss outcomes and next steps for a national action plan. They also agreed on the need for early progress, and instructed officials to continue work on the development of early actions such as addressing indirect costs of university research; the environment for biotechnology; criteria for successful federal–provincial–territorial partnering; expansion of access to venture capital; and an improved regulatory and business environment to foster innovation.

HRDC DISCUSSIONS WITH PROVINCES AND TERRITORIES

Provinces and territories are already showing leadership and taking action within their jurisdictions to meet Canada's skills and learning challenges. *Knowledge Matters* invited provinces and territories to work collaboratively with the Government of Canada to articulate a shared vision of where we want to go, and to identify actions that governments could take individually and collectively to get there.

As part of a government-to-government engagement process on *Knowledge Matters*, HRDC invited both multilateral and bilateral discussions with provinces and territories on skills and learning priorities.

Minister of Human Resources Development, Jane Stewart, discussed *Knowledge Matters* with the Council of Ministers of Education, Canada during their bi-annual meeting on April 8–10, 2002. Ministers expressed a broad interest in working together on shared priorities within the education sector. At a meeting of Deputy Ministers on the same occasion, agreement was reached on a new federal–provincial–territorial process for collaborative work on improving financial assistance for students.

Minister Stewart also discussed skills and learning at a meeting of Ministers Responsible for Social Services on May 30–31, 2002. There, Ministers committed to moving forward on a framework for a labour market strategy for persons with disabilities, and guiding work on a successor to the bilateral Employment and Assistance for Persons with Disabilities agreements. More broadly, the Ministers Responsible for Social Services agreed to focus efforts on ensuring that all Canadians have the opportunity to fully participate in the labour market, and committed to working with their sectoral colleagues, in particular their labour market colleagues, to achieve this goal.

Over the past several months, HRDC held a number of bilateral discussions with provincial and territorial ministries in the labour market, social services, and education sectors. The release of several provincial/territorial skills and learning papers has also contributed to ongoing government-to-government dialogue on skills and learning.

Discussions with provinces and territories have shown that governments largely share the same skills and learning priorities and objectives, such as improving the participation rate of underrepresented groups, and supporting essential skills development. There is also broad recognition among governments of the importance of involving all partners — businesses, labour, non-governmental organizations and educational institutions — in addressing Canada's skills challenges. A number of provinces and territories noted that government skills papers could provide a platform for increased collaboration on skills and learning priorities. Other jurisdictions emphasized the importance of ensuring that government actions are complementary, and consistent with current federal–provincial mechanisms and jurisdiction.

Next steps

HRDC is continuing to invite federal–provincial–territorial discussion on shared skills and learning priorities in the labour market, education, and social services sectors. As articulated in the September 30, 2002, Speech from the Throne, the Government of Canada is interested in working with provincial and territorial governments to ensure that Canada has the skills and learning architecture it needs to meet the challenges of the 21st century. In addition, HRDC has invited provinces and territories to collaborate with the federal government on individual skills and learning priorities.

CHAPTER 10

OVERVIEW OF DIFFERENT PERSPECTIVES AND SHARED PRIORITIES

DIFFERENT PERSPECTIVES

The engagement process for *Canada's Innovation Strategy* reached out to a very broad range of organizations, institutions and individuals. The concerns, suggestions and impressions of the various groups were shaped by different economic and social circumstances, established policies and priorities, and a host of other factors. In other words, participants in each stream viewed Canada's innovation challenge, and their role within it, through their own eyes.

Understandably, the input from regions and communities was also shaped by local circumstances. Participants from large urban centres tended to emphasize the challenges of access to sufficient long-term funding and venture capital to accelerate R&D and commercialization. They also recognized the importance of aligning the learning system to reflect local labour market conditions. Input from smaller communities focussed on basic infrastructure requirements and broadband connectivity, more opportunities for youth to stem out-migration, and incentives to retain skilled people. The differences in regional and community perspectives preclude a "one size fits all" approach to innovation.

Not surprisingly, young people were most concerned with the skills and learning aspects of innovation. They look to their own future and ask: "Will we be able to acquire the knowledge and skills we need to prosper in the knowledge-based economy?" They were worried about the accessibility of post-secondary education, but also whether schools and universities are equipping students with the full range of skills they will need to succeed in the labour force. They also emphasized the need for better access to information on a broader range of career choices, at all levels of education.

The Aboriginal community viewed innovation less as a research or commercialization concept, and more in social policy terms. From their perspective, the challenge is to bring living standards and education levels up to the point where Aboriginal people and communities can begin to participate in the knowledge-based economy. Therefore, their priority was on learning foundations, and social and community infrastructure.

> "*Innovation is not something we can produce through force — it is a state of mind and a behavioural approach.*"
>
> Aluminium Association of Canada

As the primary producer of knowledge and skills acquisition in Canada, the academic community is a vitally important driver of innovation. However, after facing many funding pressures, this community suggests that governments provide additional funds to restore depleted infrastructure, add new research and teaching capacity, and ensure that post-secondary education remains accessible to all Canadians. Universities focussed on increased research funding, including a permanent program to cover indirect costs of research. Universities also acknowledged that they must play a greater role in the commercialization of knowledge and wealth creation. This will take more of a partnership approach with industry and government. Colleges called for increased opportunities for fuller participation in the *Innovation Strategy*. Libraries stressed the importance of their role in improving community access to digital information.

More than any other group, national business associations drew a link between the fiscal climate and the pace of innovation. They wanted to review current incentives for R&D and venture capital formation, and eliminate programs that are not achieving results; they also urged that any new incentives be performance-linked and delivered through the tax system rather than new program spending. Economic development organizations see themselves as uniquely placed to drive innovation at the community level. Their view of the innovation challenge centred on the need to move the levers that generate the financial and human resources required to stimulate R&D, technology transfer and commercialization down from senior governments to the local level.

By their very nature, sector councils view innovation as a skills challenge. They have a strong track record in bringing workers, employers and educators together to increase and improve skills development in the workplace. With adequate funding from government, sector councils believed they can become stonger advocates for adult learning.

The community of small and medium-sized businesses is extremely diverse, but stood out from many other streams in expressing a sense of isolation from government and policy making. Small and medium-sized enterprises see themselves as a driving force for innovation in Canada, yet feel their potential is constrained by high taxes, regulation, and government programs and services that are tailored to large companies. One of their top concerns was access to capital and technology assistance programs. Small and medium-sized business owners sent a strong message that overly narrow eligibility criteria and complex application procedures discourage them from taking advantage of government policies and programs that support R&D, commercialization and the adoption of new technology. As a result, they believed the enormous potential for innovation among Canada's more than 2 million SMEs is underexploited. Canadians from all segments of society reinforced the need for improved access to financing for the development of innovative new firms. Also important to small and medium-sized enterprises is being able to access apprenticeships, co-ops, workplace-based training, and other lifelong learning programs.

The industry sector stream brought together a very broad range of perspectives — from traditional manufacturers and processors at one end to information technology and telecommunications and life science firms at the other. For the most part, industry sectors placed a priority on commercialization assistance, the regulatory and tax regimes, and access to an appropriately skilled work force.

The more traditional manufacturing and resource-based industries reinforced the importance of process innovations to improve productivity; emerging and highly fragmented industries, such as environmental technologies and biotechnology, stressed the need for actions that would help them mobilize into a collective force to better take advantage of global opportunities.

The events organized by HRDC gave participants with a wide range of backgrounds and experience an opportunity to interact on key issues on the skills and learning side of innovation. Despite the different perspectives they brought to the table, employers, trade union representatives, educators, Aboriginal Canadians and others agreed on many points. For most, the diagnosis expressed in the *Innovation Strategy* papers resonated strongly. They believed that skills shortages are already evident in Canada, that the impending demographic crunch threatens to make the situation worse and that a learning system designed for the industrial age will not meet Canada's needs in the knowledge-based economy. There was also strong agreement that building a learning culture in Canada is a collective responsibility, and that we will not succeed as long as the various players operate in silos and are isolated from each other.

> " *Government can support innovation, but should not be responsible for undertaking innovation. Innovation should be industry-led to ensure a market focus.* "
>
> Ocean Technology (East Coast)

SHARED PRIORITIES

As noted above, participants in each of the streams of engagement approached innovation from a particular context and perspective. However, despite enormous differences in factors such as age, region, culture, language, community size, business size and sectoral affiliation, when asked about innovation, Canadians clearly had shared priorities.

Partnerships

If there was a single overarching theme to emerge from the engagement process, it had to do with partnerships. Canadians believed that innovation performance levels, in all dimensions — economic, social, cultural or environmental — will rise or fall on the ability to forge new and stronger partnerships between and among governments, business, labour, education and training providers, and community-based organizations. At the same time, they expressed a clear sense that governments must lead the way by casting a clear vision of what a more innovative Canada might look like, and by working with all public and private sector stakeholders to translate that vision into reality.

Intergovernmental cooperation and harmonization

First and foremost, Canadians issued a strong call for cooperation and collaboration within and between the three levels of governments. All stakeholders emphasized the need for more interdepartmental coordination and cooperation. They made several recommendations regarding the positive impact on innovation performance that could be realized through harmonization of regulation, taxation, R&D support programs, and learning across levels of governments and provincial jurisdictions.

Harnessing the full potential of innovation

Many Canadians emphasized the need to look well beyond economic imperatives and to think of innovation in social and cultural terms as well. They not only saw innovation as everyone's business, but also as something that has to happen everywhere. They felt it is key to improving the quality, effectiveness and affordability of public services such as health care and education, and programs that help Canadians overcome barriers to full participation in the economy. Finally, there was a strong call for governments to recognize that innovation goes hand in hand with sustainable development and can be a vital enabling force in meeting our environmental goals.

Taking an inclusive approach to innovation

The views of many Canadians reflected the idea that *Canada's Innovation Strategy* places too much emphasis on high technology, big cities and the "new economy." They called on the government to recognize the enormous potential for productivity-enhancing innovation in traditional manufacturing, processing and natural resource industries, which are so important to the economic vibrancy and quality of life in Canada's regions.

There was a similar call for a more inclusive approach to skills development that focusses beyond "advanced technical and scientific skills." Overall, participants felt that we can no longer afford, as a society, to "devalue" the work of tradespeople. Participants from different regions, sectors and occupations emphasized that serious skills shortages are now emerging in the skilled trades. Employers, educators and community leaders also stressed the need for young people to gain vitally important business, management and entrepreneurial skills over the course of their high school and post-secondary education. They were unanimous in calling for more "hands on" learning opportunities, including apprenticeships, internships, "mentorships" and co-op assignments, to better align the learning system with the labour market.

Another issue that surfaced during the engagement process had to do with barriers that keep talented people on the sidelines of the labour market. Canadians were critical of "protectionist" trades and professional associations, and provincial licensing bodies that do not respect legitimate foreign credentials. Restrictions that prevent highly skilled and educated immigrants from getting to work soon after arriving in Canada, they said, must be lifted.

While recognizing the central role that immigration will play in meeting future skill requirements, many people felt that the country's first priority should be to invest in the skills of Canadians and, in particular, to bring Aboriginal people, persons with disabilities, and older workers into the mainstream of the work force. There was also a concern that the *Innovation Strategy* did not adequately address growing affordability problems regarding post-secondary education and adult learning, especially if the goals are to substantially increase the number of adult learners and high-school learners who pursue post-secondary studies. There was a high level of concurrence that greater efforts should be made to ensure accessible learning paths for Canadians. Enhanced opportunities for e-learning, increased commitment from employers for work-place-based training, and higher levels of collaboration among learning providers, particularly universities and colleges, were all presented as priorities for action. There was strong agreement that employers must change current attitudes and look upon expenditures for workplace training as investments, not costs. At the same time, most participants saw a necessary role for government in underwriting training costs, perhaps through tax credits, incentives or creative uses of employment insurance funds. Academic leaders called for improvements to financial assistance for adult, part-time, Aboriginal and other learners. It was also noted that as long as there are Canadians who cannot meet their basic needs, they will not pursue the learning opportunities required for success and mobility at work. Thus, "social inclusiveness" and "labour market inclusiveness" go hand in hand.

Supporting community capacity and clusters

Delivering universal broadband access to communities in all regions was, arguably, the most frequently mentioned specific initiative to improve Canada's innovation performance. If governments are prepared to provide modern infrastructure, including world-class transportation links and high-speed broadband networks, there was a strong feeling that communities across Canada would be able to pool capital and human resources, and participate in world-class innovation activities.

Participants talked a good deal about the *Innovation Strategy*'s objective of developing 10 internationally recognized technology "clusters" in Canada. However, there was little consensus on this target, and much discussion about how clusters emerge and how communities could apply the cluster concept to improve their capacity to become "magnets for investment and talent." They argued that clusters could be "virtual," as well as geographically or sector-based. Stronger learning networks and linkages between R&D institutions and private sector businesses were seen as key elements.

> *"Innovation will definitely shake up our industrial infrastructure, and with it our economic paradigm."*
>
> Canadian Industry Program for Energy Conservation

Expanding the knowledge base to support innovation and learning

Throughout the engagement process, participants noted gaps in the information available, whether in reference to the most effective approaches to basic skills development, workplace training, adult education, e-learning and apprenticeship, how much capacity universities and colleges actually have, where and how R&D dollars are being invested across the country, or how to measure the impact of cluster approaches. The opportunity to share best practices across the country was a priority for most groups. Many thought that governments should lead the way in compiling and disseminating various kinds of information. In the area of labour market issues, sector councils were widely seen as well placed to play a coordinating role; in other areas, participants felt that new coordinating mechanisms may have to be developed.

The need for culture change

Another message from many participants was that Canada's innovation challenge is a cultural issue, at the root of which lies a need to change the mindset of Canadians with regard to risk, reward and success. Many believed this process should begin in K-12 schools, and that efforts should be made to introduce young people to creative business concepts. There was also wide support for a collaborative effort to raise awareness and pride in our innovation achievements and to brand Canada as an exciting place to work, learn and invest, not only for foreigners, but for Canadians. This need for a stronger culture of innovation was seen as permeating all segments of Canadian society — governments, education institutions, R&D laboratories, corporations and communities.

Moving forward faster

Given the range of interests and perspectives represented in the engagement process, there was a surprising level of support for the analysis, policy directions and milestones set out in *Achieving Excellence* and *Knowledge Matters*. At the same time, one of the clearest messages to come from individuals, organizations and institutions in all regions and sectors was, simply put, to get on with the job. Whether in relation to regulatory reform, encouraging venture capital formation, promoting workplace training and adult learning, overhauling immigration machinery, or revamping the K-12 and post-secondary learning systems, there was a strong sense that there has been enough discussion, the mission is clear, and the time for action is now.

HIGHLIGHTS OF SUGGESTED ACTIONS AND RECOMMENDATIONS

Around the shared priorities of Canadians there were recurring sets of mutually reinforcing recommendations for actions that seemed to cut across the full spectrum of input. These are summarized in this section.

Strengthening the learning system

All stakeholders recognized that lifelong learning and skills development are the foundations of an innovative culture, and agreed that governments must spend more wisely across the full spectrum of the learning system. There was some appetite for national standards in relation to K-12 education and training programs, but a much broader and stronger sentiment that governments should cooperate more effectively in these areas. In particular, participants felt that governments should focus on areas such as e-learning, expanding the teaching and research capacity of colleges and universities, ensuring that post-secondary education and adult learning are accessible to all Canadians, and ensuring that the skills of newcomers are fully used.

Participants supported the direction, if not always the details, behind the learning objectives and milestones set out in the *Innovation Strategy* papers. However, many took issue with the emphasis on science and technology and advanced post-secondary learning, when shortages in skilled trades and practical business management skills are already looming. They saw a similar bias in a K-12 education system that streams young people toward college and university, and away from apprenticeship and other learning paths.

To ensure accessibility to learning opportunities, many participants felt the governments should:

- address student debt issues and develop more flexible repayment options;

- extend student financial assistance programs to support part-time learning; and

- establish tax-levered personal learning accounts similar to registered retirement savings plans.

To align the learning system with the labour market, many participants called for:

- active marketing of career opportunities in the skilled trades by employers, unions and sector councils, and for these groups to supply young people, parents, teachers and guidance counselors with timely, accurate labour force information;

- greater attention to entrepreneurialism and management skills, and life skills in the high school curriculum, and greater crossover between science, engineering and business programs at the post-secondary level;

- better career planning information and career counselling for K-12 students based on timely, accurate labour force data; and

- vastly expanded co-op, internship and apprenticeship opportunities in the K-12 and post-secondary systems, and "mentorship" opportunities that begin in school and extend into work life.

"*Skills and human resources are the most critical elements within a national innovation strategy.*"

Canadian Council of Chief Executives

Building an inclusive and skilled work force

A wide range of participants noted that workers in Canada have less access to formal training than in other countries. They believed this was due, in large measure, to the fact that the vast majority of Canadians work in small and medium-sized enterprises, and that identifying training needs, projecting future skill requirements, and sourcing the right training programs and services is difficult and expensive for small companies.

Many participants in all regions recognized the importance of immigration in view of the demographic challenges Canada faces and the immediate labour force requirements for skilled tradespeople and teaching and research faculty. They were clear, however, that in meeting the future need for skills, the priority must be revamping our education and training system to upgrade the skills of Canadians. There were also many calls for a "modern," skills-based immigration system featuring a faster approval process and measures that will speed up entrance into the labour force and ensure full application of skills and abilities.

To increase Canada's workplace training efforts, many participants felt individuals and employers should be encouraged to do more, with:

- tax credits that would stimulate more employer-sponsored training and encourage individuals to participate in lifelong learning;

- increased funding to sector councils so they can extend their strategic human resource management services to SMEs; and

- increased corporate investment in employee training and development programs.

To improve the contribution of the immigration system to Canada's skill needs, many participants felt that:

- provincial licensing bodies and professional associations should recognize foreign credentials and the skills of foreign-trained workers;

- prior learning assessment and recognition services should be provided through sector councils and colleges to speed the integration of new arrivals into the labour market;

- governments and learning institutions should make it easier and more affordable for foreign students to come to Canada and to apply for permanent residency upon completion of their studies;

- employers and sector councils should be more involved in recruiting skilled immigrants; and

- changes should be made to the immigration system to facilitate immigration approval processes, especially for skilled persons.

Enhancing the innovation environment

Industry champions spanning all sectors of the economy believed that the innovation environment is improving, but that Canada does not yet offer the "visible" advantages that will attract R&D investments by multinational corporations. Nor do they believe that Canada offers the right mix of incentives and supports to help small and medium-sized enterprises substantially increase their investments in innovation. They called on federal, provincial and municipal governments to concentrate on ensuring that Canada has world-class infrastructure, including transportation links and high-speed networks that support innovation; to provide clear, stable and coherent policies that support innovation; and to lead by example in developing innovative approaches to regulation, policy making and delivery of services.

To improve the innovation environment, many participants felt that:

- governments should work with industry, consumers and others to complete a thorough, sector-by-sector regulatory review by 2005 — at a minimum, to streamline regulatory regimes between domestic jurisdictions, and harmonize product acceptance codes and other regulations and standards with major trading partners;

- capital taxes should be eliminated and employment insurance premiums reduced;

- the Government of Canada should make scientific research and experimental development tax credits refundable and readily accessible to firms in all sectors, particularly to small and medium-sized enterprises;

- tax incentives should be offered to encourage firms to apply productivity-enhancing technologies;

- copyright law should be reviewed to strike a balance between creators' rights and users' rights that is suited to a digital economy; and

- more information should be provided about the management of intellectual property for academic researchers and small and medium-sized enterprises, and that the intellectual property and patent regime should be modernized to simplify processes and reduce approval times.

Improving research, development and commercialization

While agreeing on the need to create and apply knowledge much more vigorously, many participants questioned whether joining the top five in the world R&D rankings is a realistic goal for Canada. Still, their message was clear — Canada must spend more and spend smarter to stimulate basic and applied research, turn research professionals into "innovation managers," increase the supply of venture capital to small and medium-sized enterprises, and encourage innovation with more support for the application and use of productivity-enhancing technologies and processes.

To promote R&D, many participants felt that:

- the roles of governments, industries, and universities and colleges in R&D should be clarified, and that all these stakeholders should work more collaboratively to increase the levels of both basic and applied research;

- funding should be more widely available for federal granting councils to support research in colleges and technical institutes;

- the indirect costs of federally sponsored research should be financed, and the deferred maintenance and capacity issues in universities and colleges should be addressed;

- mechanisms should be created to coordinate and set priorities for federally funded R&D; and to share facilities, technical and management personnel among industries, universities and government departments; and

- the science capacity of federal departments and agencies should be rebuilt.

To promote commercialization, many participants felt governments should:

- boost funding and broaden eligibility criteria for the Canada Foundation for Innovation, Industrial Research Assistance Program, Technology Early Action Measures and Technology Partnerships Canada, and simplify application procedures to make them more "small and medium-sized enterprise-friendly;"

- create an internship program to help university researchers acquire the full range of innovation management skills;

- showcase and support Canadian technology products through government procurement;

- consider mandate changes for the Business Development Bank of Canada and Export Development Canada, or the creation of new institutions to improve the supply of venture capital; and

- provide more incentives to private sector firms for commercialization activities.

To increase access to capital, many participants called for:

- the development of a critical mass of knowledgeable investors in the venture capital community; and

- incentives to increase the supply of angel investment and venture capital for innovative small firms and in smaller urban centres.

Strengthening communities

Participants across all groups and sectors in the engagement process stressed the need to attend to the basic infrastructure requirements (such as roads, schools and hospitals) that underpin the ability of communities to develop and harness their innovation potential, and to provide the quality of life that attracts and keeps highly skilled workers. In many cases, participants stressed the need to build the capacity of municipal governments to participate fully in a national *Innovation Strategy* in order to ensure that local needs are addressed and local assets are fully leveraged.

There was consensus across many streams that, rather than concentrating on the goal of creating 10 geographically based innovation clusters, which risks spreading available capital and resources too thinly, governments should focus on creating a positive regulatory and taxation environment so that clusters can emerge on their own. Smaller communities called for greater emphasis on innovation enabling "connective" infrastructure, so that people and businesses, no matter where they are located, can participate in "virtual" innovation clusters. These communities also stressed the importance of access to public and social infrastructure, e-learning, and workplace-based training opportunities. This reaction was particularly pronounced in rural and Aboriginal communities.

To strengthen and build more innovative communities in Canada, participants called for:

- broadband connectivity in all regions and communities, and affordable access to high-speed networks that will not only support new business opportunities, but also new ways of accessing learning, health care and other public services;

- efforts to enhance the capacities of local governments, particularly in technical and financial fields, so that they can play a stronger role in enabling innovation at the community level;

- tax policies that enhance the competitiveness of smaller communities and regions;

- attention to stimulating innovation in traditional industries such as mining, forestry and heavy manufacturing;

- efforts to mobilize smaller communities in developing their own innovation and learning strategies; and

- efforts to address basic quality of life and learning issues confronting Aboriginal people.

" ... *the* Innovation Strategy *needs to be more than a passing policy trend, but an essential theme for many years. This theme needs to penetrate the decision making of all departments, all levels of government, the private sector, academia and other stakeholders for decades to fully take root.*"

Natural Resources Canada Advisory Board on Energy Science and Technology

CANADA'S INNOVATION STRATEGY: GOALS AND PROPOSED ACTIONS

I. *ACHIEVING EXCELLENCE: INVESTING IN PEOPLE, KNOWLEDGE AND OPPORTUNITY*

THE KNOWLEDGE PERFORMANCE CHALLENGE

The Government of Canada proposes the following goals, targets and federal priorities to help more firms develop, adopt and market leading-edge innovations.

Goals

- Vastly increase public and private investments in knowledge infrastructure to improve Canada's R&D performance.

- Ensure that a growing number of firms benefit from the commercial application of knowledge.

Targets

- By 2010, rank among the top five countries in the world in terms of R&D performance.

- By 2010, at least double the Government of Canada's current investments in R&D.

- By 2010, rank among world leaders in the share of private sector sales from new innovations.

- By 2010, raise venture capital investments per capita to prevailing U.S. levels.

Government of Canada Priorities

1. Address key challenges for the university research environment. The Government of Canada has committed to implementing the following initiatives:

   - Support the indirect costs of university research. Contribute to a portion of the indirect costs of federally supported research, taking into account the particular situation of smaller universities.

   - Leverage the commercialization potential of publicly funded academic research. Support academic institutions in identifying intellectual property with commercial potential and forging partnerships with the private sector to commercialize research results.

   - Provide internationally competitive research opportunities in Canada. Increase support to the granting councils to enable them to award more research grants at higher funding levels.

2. Renew the Government of Canada's science and technology capacity to respond to emerging public policy, stewardship and economic challenges and opportunities.

- The Government of Canada will consider a collaborative approach to investing in research in order to focus federal capacity on emerging science-based issues and opportunities. The government would build collaborative networks across government departments, universities, non-governmental organizations and the private sector.

3. Encourage innovation and the commercialization of knowledge in the private sector.

- Provide greater incentives for the commercialization of world-first innovations. The Government of Canada will consider increased support for established commercialization programs that target investments in biotechnology, information and communications technologies, sustainable energy, mining and forestry, advanced materials and manufacturing, aquaculture and eco-efficiency.

- Provide more incentives to small and medium-sized enterprises to adopt and develop leading-edge innovations. The Government of Canada will consider providing support to the National Research Council Canada's Industrial Research Assistance Program to help Canadian small and medium-sized enterprises assess and access global technology, form international R&D alliances, and establish international technology-based ventures.

- Reward Canada's innovators. The Government of Canada will consider implementing a new and prestigious national award, given annually, to recognize internationally competitive innovators in Canada's private sector.

- Increase the supply of venture capital in Canada. The Business Development Bank of Canada will pool the assets of various partners, invest these proceeds in smaller, specialized venture capital funds and manage the portfolio on behalf of its limited partners.

THE SKILLS CHALLENGE

The Government of Canada proposes the following goals, targets and federal priorities to develop, attract and retain the highly qualified people required to fuel Canada's innovation performance.

Goals

- Develop the most skilled and talented labour force in the world.

- Ensure that Canada receives the skilled immigrants it needs and helps immigrants to achieve their full potential in the Canadian labour market and society.

Targets

- Over the next five years, increase the number of adults pursuing learning opportunities by one million.

- Through to 2010, increase the admission of master's and PhD students at Canadian universities by an average of five percent per year.

- By 2002, implement the new *Immigration and Refugee Protection Act* and regulations.

- By 2004, significantly improve Canada's performance in the recruitment of foreign talent, including foreign students, by means of both the permanent immigrant and the temporary foreign workers programs.

Government of Canada Priorities

1. Produce new graduates. The Government of Canada will consider the following initiatives:

   - Provide financial incentives to students registered in graduate studies programs, and double the number of master's and doctoral fellowships and scholarships awarded by the federal granting councils.

   - Create a world-class scholarship program of the same prestige and scope as the Rhodes Scholarship; support and facilitate a coordinated international student recruitment strategy led by Canadian universities; and implement changes to immigration policies and procedures to facilitate the retention of international students.

   - Establish a cooperative research program to support graduate and post-graduate students and, in special circumstances, undergraduates, wishing to combine formal academic training with extensive applied research experience in a work setting.

2. Modernize the Canadian immigration system. The Government of Canada has committed to:

   - Maintain its commitment to higher immigration levels and work toward increasing the number of highly skilled workers.

   - Expand the capacity, agility and presence of the domestic and overseas immigration delivery system to offer competitive service standards for skilled workers, both permanent and temporary.

   - Brand Canada as a destination of choice for skilled workers.

   - Use a redesigned temporary foreign worker program and expanded provincial nominee agreements to facilitate the entry of highly skilled workers, and to ensure that the benefits of immigration are more evenly distributed across the country.

THE INNOVATION ENVIRONMENT CHALLENGE

The Government of Canada proposes the following goals, targets and federal priorities to protect Canadians and encourage them to adopt innovations; encourage firms to invest in innovation; and attract the people and capital upon which innovation depends.

Goals

- Address potential public and business confidence challenges before they develop.

- Ensure that Canada's stewardship regimes and marketplace framework policies are world-class.

- Improve incentives for innovation.

- Ensure that Canada is recognized as a leading innovative country.

Targets

- By 2010, complete systematic expert reviews of Canada's most important business and regulatory regimes.

- Ensure Canada's business taxation regime continues to be competitive with those of other G-7 countries.

- By 2005, substantially improve Canada's profile with international investors.

- By 2004, fully implement the Council of Science and Technology Advisors' guidelines to ensure the effective use of science and technology in government decision making.

Government of Canada Priorities

1. Ensure effective decision making for new and existing policies and regulatory priorities. The Government of Canada will consider the following initiatives:

   - Support "Canadian Academies of Science" to build on and complement the contribution of existing Canadian science organizations.

   - Undertake systematic expert reviews of existing stewardship regimes through international benchmarking, and collaborate internationally to address shared challenges.

2. Ensure that Canada's business taxation regime is internationally competitive.

   - The Government of Canada will work with the provinces and territories to ensure that Canada's federal, provincial and territorial tax systems encourage and support innovation.

3. Brand Canada as a location of choice for investors.

   - The Government of Canada has committed to a sustained investment branding strategy. This could include Investment Team Canada missions and targeted promotional activities.

COMMUNITY-BASED INNOVATION CHALLENGES

The Government of Canada proposes the following goals, targets and federal priorities to support innovation in communities across the country.

Goals

- Governments at all levels work together to stimulate the creation of more clusters of innovation at the community level.

- Federal, provincial/territorial and municipal governments cooperate and supplement their current efforts to unleash the full innovation potential of communities across Canada, guided by community-based assessments of local strengths, weaknesses and opportunities.

Targets

- By 2010, develop at least 10 internationally recognized technology clusters.

- By 2010, significantly improve the innovation performance of communities across Canada.

- By 2005, ensure that high-speed broadband access is widely available to Canadian communities.

Government of Canada Priorities

1. Support the development of globally competitive industrial clusters.

   - The Government of Canada will accelerate community-based consultations already under way to develop technology clusters where Canada has the potential to develop world-class expertise, and identify and start more clusters.

2. Strengthen the innovation performance of communities.

   - The Government of Canada will consider providing funding to smaller communities to enable them to develop innovation strategies tailored to their unique circumstances. Communities would be expected to engage local leaders from the academic, private and public sectors in formulating their innovation strategies. Additional resources, drawing on existing and new programs, could be provided to implement successful community innovation strategies.

   - As part of this effort, the Government of Canada will work with industry, the provinces and territories, communities, and the public to advance a private sector solution to further the deployment of broadband, particularly for rural and remote areas.

II. *KNOWLEDGE MATTERS: SKILLS AND LEARNING FOR CANADIANS*

CHILDREN AND YOUTH

Goal

To give our children and youth the best possible start in life.

Milestones

- Canada becomes one of the top three countries in mathematics, science and reading achievement.

- All young Canadians are computer and Internet literate by grade school graduation.

- All students who graduate from high school achieve a level of literacy sufficient to participate in the knowledge-based economy.

- The proportion of high school graduates who have a working knowledge of both official languages doubles.

How the Government of Canada Could Contribute

The Government of Canada will consider actions in a number of areas to better support children and youth. These actions will be discussed with provincial and territorial governments and with stakeholders:

1. Support early childhood development programs and services. Implement the commitments of the 2001 Budget regarding Aboriginal children. In partnership with provincial and territorial governments, continue to implement the commitments in the Early Childhood Development Agreement.

2. Improve education outcomes of on-reserve First Nations children and youth. Work with partners to find ways of improving First Nations education outcomes in on-reserve schools.

3. Help young Canadians make a successful transition from school to work. Examine ways to improve the Government of Canada's Youth Employment Strategy to better assist youth in succeeding in the labour market.

POST-SECONDARY EDUCATION

Goal

All qualified Canadians have access to high-quality post-secondary education.

Milestones

- One hundred percent of high school graduates have the opportunity to participate in some form of post-secondary education.

- Over the next decade, 50 percent of 25–64 year olds, including an increased proportion of individuals from at-risk groups, have a post-secondary credential (up from the current 39 percent).

- Over the next decade, the number of apprentices completing a certification program doubles (to 37 000).

- Admission of master's and PhD students at Canadian universities increases by an average of 5 percent per year through to 2010.

How the Government of Canada Could Contribute

The Government will consider actions in a number of areas related to post-secondary education. These actions will be discussed with provincial and territorial governments and with stakeholders:

1. Make post-secondary education more financially accessible to low-income Canadians. Work with provinces and territories to ensure the effective implementation of the changes to the Canada Study Grants for students with disabilities. Examine further improvements to student financial assistance to better support students in need and to encourage them to enrol in post-secondary education.

2. Encourage low-income and moderate-income Canadians currently in the work force to participate in post-secondary education by "learning while they earn." Improve student financial assistance programs to help working Canadians upgrade their education through part-time study.

3. Facilitate mobility and access to post-secondary education for adult learners and students. Explore with provinces and territories how best to enhance the mobility of students and adult learners by facilitating the transfer of credits among institutions, and the recognition of prior learning and experience.

4. Encourage Canadians to look to skilled trades for employment. Discuss with partners possible means of encouraging more Canadians to consider working in the skilled trades.

5. Build on the expertise of community colleges. Explore how to help support the important role played by community colleges in equipping Canadians with the skills they need for the future.

6. Increase the number of highly qualified people. Discuss with partners and stakeholders how best to increase the number of highly qualified people available to drive innovation in Canada's economy.

ADULT LABOUR FORCE

Goal

To ensure Canada's current and emerging work force is more highly skilled and adaptable.

Milestones

- Within five years, the number of adult learners increases by one million men and women throughout all segments of society.

- Within five years, businesses increase by one third their annual investment in training per employee.

- The number of adult Canadians with low literacy skills is reduced by 25 percent over the next decade.

How the Government of Canada Could Contribute

The Government will consider actions in a number of areas to help Canadians pursue learning opportunities and realize their aspirations, and increase our supply of labour. These actions will be discussed with provincial and territorial governments and with stakeholders:

1. Increase the reach and scope of sector council activities. Work with sector councils to increase the number of sectors covered, as well as expand human resource planning and skills development within sectors and small and medium-sized businesses. Discuss with sector councils and other partners the development of a cross-sectoral "Workplace Skills Development Gold Standard" to recognize firms that engage in exemplary learning programs.

2. Support the development and dissemination of knowledge and information on adult learning. Examine ways to further research and the development and dissemination of knowledge and information about adult skills and learning.

3. Encourage workplace-based learning and opportunities for workers to "learn while they earn." Examine with partners possible financial incentives for employers who support essential skills development for their employees. Examine possible enhancements to student assistance programs for part-time study.

4. Ensure the best use of resources for active labour market measures. Building on current labour market development partnerships, work with provinces and territories to ensure the most effective use of resources to meet the skills development needs of Canadians in our evolving labour market.

5. Encourage the participation of those facing barriers to labour market participation. Consider, in cooperation with provinces and territories and other partners, targeted skills development initiatives to help persons with disabilities, Aboriginal people, visible minorities, individuals with low levels of literacy or foundation skills, and others facing particular barriers to participation in the labour market.

IMMIGRATION

Goal

To ensure that Canada continues to attract the highly skilled immigrants it needs and helps them to achieve their full potential in Canadian society and the labour market.

Milestones

- By 2010, 65 percent (up from 58 percent in 2000) of adult immigrants have post-secondary education.

- The income gap between immigrants in the work force and Canadian-born workers with comparable skills and education is reduced by 50 percent.

How the Government of Canada Could Contribute

The Government will consider actions that will be discussed with provincial and territorial governments and with stakeholders, taking into account the sharing of responsibilities under federal–provincial agreements relating to immigration:

1. Attracting and selecting highly skilled immigrants. Examine, with provinces, territories, municipal governments, employers and other partners, how best to ensure that Canada continues to receive the skilled immigrants it needs.

2. Developing an integrated and transparent approach to the recognition of foreign credentials. Work in collaboration with provinces and territories, regulatory bodies, employers and other stakeholders to develop fair, transparent and consistent processes to assess and recognize foreign qualifications before and after arrival.

3. Better supporting the integration of immigrants into Canada's labour market. Examine, with provinces and territories and other partners, ways to help immigrants integrate successfully into the labour market, including language training, job-related initiatives with employers, and better labour market information and job search assistance.

4. Helping immigrants to achieve their full potential over the course of their working lives. Examine ways to ensure that Canada has the necessary information and understanding to maximize the labour force benefits of immigration to our economy and society over the long term.